PHOTO ERROR

Please note the following correction on page 33 of *Basic Wiring & Electrical Repairs:*

In how-to step #10 a **gas** water heater thermostat is pictured instead of an **electric** water heater thermostat.

However, the directions for step #10 are accurate and safe, and do apply to an electric water heater thermostat.

The publisher apologizes for any inconvenience this erroneous photo may cause you.

BLACK & DECKER®

HOME IMPROVEMENT LIBRARY™

Basic Wiring & Electrical Repairs

Cy DeCosse Incorporated
Minnetonka, Minnesota

Contents

Introduction to Electricity

Wiring Basics

Wall Switches

o'o9

Also available from the publisher:
*Everyday Home Repairs, Decorating with
Paint & Wallcovering, Carpentry: Tools•
Shelves•Walls•Doors, Kitchen Remodeling,
Building Decks, Home Plumbing Projects
& Repairs*

Library of Congress
Cataloging-in-Publication Data

Basic wiring & electrical repairs

p. cm.— (Black & Decker home
improvement library)
Includes index.
ISBN 0-86573-714-2.
ISBN 0-86573-715-0 (pbk.)
1. Electric wiring, Interior—Amateurs'
manuals.
I. Title: Basic wiring and electrical repairs.
II. Series.
TK9901.B39 1990   90-42688
621.319'24—dc20   CIP

CY DECOSSE INCORPORATED
Chairman: Cy DeCosse
President: James B. Maus
Executive Vice President: William B. Jones

Created by: The Editors of Cy DeCosse
Incorporated, in cooperation with Black &
Decker. **BLACK&DECKER** is a trademark
of the Black & Decker Corporation, and is
used under license.

Receptacles

Light Fixtures

Doorbells & Thermostats

Inspector's Notebook 110

Index 126

Project Director: John Riha
Senior Art Director: Tim Himsel
Editor: Bryan Trandem
Project Manager: Dianne Talmage
Technical Production Editor: Paul Currie
Copy Editors: Janice Cauley, Bernie
   Maehren, Claire Taylor
Art Director: Dave Schelitzche
Director of Development, Planning & Production: Jim Bindas
Production Manager: Amelia Merz
Shop Supervisor: Greg Wallace
Prop Stylist: Jim Huntley

Electronic Publishing Analyst: Kevin D. Frakes
Production Staff: Joe Fahey, Melissa
   Grabanski, Mark Jacobson, Yelena
   Konrardy, Daniel Meyers, Linda Schloegel,
   Nik Wogstad

Studio Manager: Rebecca DaWald
Photographers: Phil Aarrestad, Kim Baily,
   Paul Englund, Rex Irmen, John Lauenstein,
   Bill Lindner, Mark Macemon, Charles
   Nields, Mette Nielsen, Mike Parker,
   Cathleen Shannon

Contributing Editors: Greg Breining,
   Kathleen Childers

Technical Consultants: Al Hildenbrand (Al's
   Electric Works), Marty Kumm, Jim Stumpfa
   (North Side Electric), Robert Weaver
   (Weaver Electric)

Contributing Manufacturers: Cooper
   Industries, Honeywell Corporation,
   Northern States Power Company,
   Waxman Industries, Inc.

Color Separations: Scantrans
Printing: R. R. Donnelley & Sons (1290)

Introduction

Basic Wiring & Electrical Repairs is a complete guide to fixing and maintaining your home's electrical system. Clear, concise language and hundreds of close-up, color photographs lead you through every step of the repair process. Throughout this book, your safety is given first consideration.

Making electrical repairs is not difficult. The simple safety procedures outlined in this book, together with common sense, can remove any doubts you might have about do-it-yourself electrical repairs. You'll discover that home electrical projects are safe, easy, and satisfying. In addition, you can save hundreds of dollars over the cost of hiring a professional electrician.

The opening pages of this book describe how electricity works. You'll learn how electricity enters the home, how it is distributed to different rooms, and how grounding the system keeps it safe. A glossary provides a handy reference for the electrical terms used in this book, and a catalog of tools helps you identify the hand tools, power tools, and specialty tools needed for electrical repairs.

The next section is an overview of the parts of an electrical system. It includes a wealth of information on how to identify cable and wire types, strip wires, make failure-proof connections, estimate the capacity of your present system, calculate the load on individual circuits, make a valuable map of your circuits, and install junction boxes. We've also included many photographs of older parts to help you identify the age of your wiring system and anticipate possible repairs.

Next is a carefully planned section of repair projects. Every detail of identifying and repairing switches, receptacles, fluorescent and incandescent lights, thermostats, doorbells, and plugs is completely outlined and photographed, and every step has been reviewed by technical experts for accuracy and safety.

Finally, we have identified some of the most common electrical code violations and potential problems that may be found in any household electrical system, especially older ones. These problems and their solutions are organized into a special section at the end of the book called the "Inspector's Notebook." The "Inspector's Notebook" is like having a professional electrician at your side to point out any problems that might not be readily apparent to the average homeowner. This special section makes sure that your electrical system will always be well maintained and in safe working condition.

Basic Wiring & Electrical Repairs is the product of many long hours of research and development. We're proud to offer this book as a valuable addition to your home improvement library.

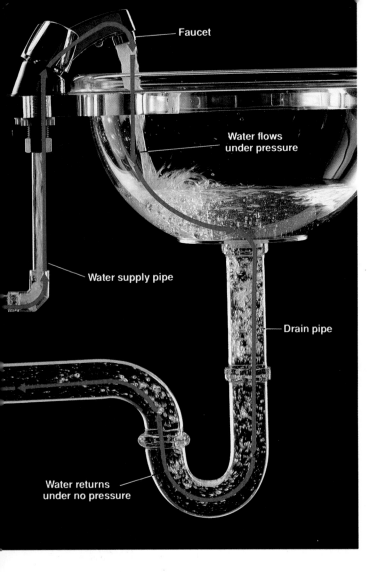

Faucet

Water flows
under pressure

Water supply pipe

Drain pipe

Water returns
under no pressure

Understanding Electricity

A household electrical system can be compared with a home's plumbing system. Electrical current flows in wires in much the same way that water flows inside pipes. Both electricity and water enter the home, are distributed throughout the house, do their "work," and then exit.

In plumbing, water first flows through the pressurized water supply system. In electricity, current first flows along hot wires. Current flowing along hot wires also is pressurized. The pressure of electrical current is called **voltage.**

Large supply pipes can carry a greater volume of water than small pipes. Likewise, large electrical wires carry more current than small wires. This current-carrying capacity of wires is called **amperage.**

Water is made available for use through the faucets, spigots, and shower heads in a home. Electricity is made available through receptacles, switches, and fixtures.

Water finally leaves the home through a drain system, which is not pressurized. Similarly, electrical current flows back through neutral wires. The current in neutral wires is not pressurized, and is said to be at zero voltage.

White (neutral) wire

Current returns
under no pressure

Switch

Light fixture

Black (hot) wire

Current flows
under pressure

Glossary of Electrical Terms

ampere (or **amp**): Refers to the rate at which electrical power flows to a light, tool, or an appliance.

armored cable: Two or more wires that are grouped together and protected by a flexible metal covering.

box: A device used to contain wiring connections.

BX: See **armored cable.**

cable: Two or more wires that are grouped together and protected by a covering or sheath.

circuit: A continuous loop of electrical current flowing along wires or cables.

circuit breaker: A safety device that interrupts an electrical circuit in the event of an overload or short circuit.

conductor: Any material that allows electrical current to flow through it. Copper wire is an especially good conductor.

conduit: A metal or plastic tube used to protect wires.

continuity: An uninterrupted electrical pathway through a circuit or electrical fixture.

current: The movement of electrons along a conductor.

duplex receptacle: A receptacle that provides connections for two plugs.

feed wire: A conductor that carries 120-volt current uninterrupted from the service panel.

fuse: A safety device, usually found in older homes, that interrupts electrical circuits during an overload or short circuit.

Greenfield: See **armored cable.**

grounded wire: See **neutral wire.**

grounding wire: A wire used in an electrical circuit to conduct current to the earth in the event of a short circuit. The grounding wire often is a bare copper wire.

hot wire: Any wire that carries voltage. In an electrical circuit, the hot wire usually is covered with black or red insulation.

insulator: Any material, such as plastic or rubber, that resists the flow of electrical current. Insulating materials protect wires and cables.

junction box: See **box.**

meter: A device used to measure the amount of electrical power being used.

neutral wire: A wire that returns current at zero voltage to the source of electrical power. Usually covered with white or light gray insulation. Also called the grounded wire.

outlet: See **receptacle.**

overload: A demand for more current than the circuit wires or electrical device was designed to carry. Usually causes a fuse to blow or a circuit breaker to trip.

pigtail: A short wire used to connect two or more circuit wires to a single screw terminal.

polarized receptacle: A receptacle designed to keep hot current flowing along black or red wires, and neutral current flowing along white or gray wires.

power: The result of hot current flowing for a period of time. Use of power makes heat, motion, or light.

receptacle: A device that provides plug-in access to electrical power.

Romex: A brand name of plastic-sheathed electrical cable that is commonly used for indoor wiring.

screw terminal: A place where a wire connects to a receptacle, switch, or fixture.

service panel: A metal box usually near the site where electrical power enters the house. In the service panel, electrical current is split into individual circuits. The service panel has circuit breakers or fuses to protect each circuit.

short circuit: An accidental and improper contact between two current-carrying wires, or between a current-carrying wire and a grounding conductor.

switch: A device that controls electrical current passing through hot circuit wires. Used to turn lights and appliances on and off.

UL: An abbreviation for Underwriters Laboratories, an organization that tests electrical devices and manufactured products for safety.

voltage (or **volts**): A measurement of electricity in terms of pressure.

wattage (or **watt**): A measurement of electrical power in terms of total energy consumed. Watts can be calculated by multiplying the voltage times the amps.

wire nut: A device used to connect two or more wires together.

Electricity & Safety

Safety should be the primary concern of anyone working with electricity. Although most household electrical repairs are simple and straightforward, always use caution and good judgment when working with electrical wiring or devices. Common sense can prevent accidents.

The basic rule of electrical safety is: **Always turn off power to the area or device you are working on.** At the main service panel, remove the fuse or shut off the circuit breaker that controls the circuit you are servicing. Then check to make sure

the power is off by testing for power with a neon circuit tester (page 18). Restore power only when the repair or replacement project is complete.

Follow the safety tips shown on these pages. Never attempt an electrical project beyond your skill or confidence level. Never attempt to repair or replace your main service panel or service entrance head (pages 12 to 13). These are jobs for a qualified electrician, and require that the power company shuts off power to your house.

Shut off power to the proper circuit at the fuse box or main service panel before beginning work.

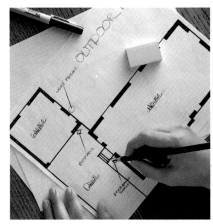

Make a map of your household electrical circuits (pages 30 to 33) to help you turn the proper circuits on and off for electrical repairs.

Close service panel door and post a warning sign to prevent others from turning on power while you are working on electrical projects.

Keep a flashlight near your main service panel. Check flashlight batteries regularly.

Always check for power at the fixture you are servicing before you begin any work.

Use only UL approved electrical parts or devices. These devices have been tested for safety by Underwriters Laboratories.

Wear rubber-soled shoes while working on electrical projects. On damp floors, stand on a rubber mat or dry wooden boards.

Use fiberglass or wood ladders when making routine household repairs near the service head.

Use GFCI receptacles (ground-fault circuit-interrupters) where specified by local electrical codes (pages 74 to 77).

Protect children with receptacle caps or childproof receptacle covers (page 69).

Use extension cords only for temporary connections. Never place them underneath rugs, or fasten them to walls, baseboards, or other surfaces.

Use correct fuses or breakers in the main service panel (pages 28 to 29). Never install a fuse or breaker that has a higher amperage rating than the circuit wires.

Do not touch metal pipes, faucets, or fixtures while working with electricity. The metal may provide a grounding path, allowing electrical current to flow through your body.

Never alter the prongs of a plug to fit a receptacle. If possible, install a new grounded receptacle.

Do not drill walls or ceilings without first shutting off electrical power to the circuits that may be hidden. Use double-insulated tools.

Your Electrical System

Electrical power that enters the home is produced by large **power plants**. Power plants are located in all parts of the country, and generate electricity with turbines that are turned by water, wind, or steam. From these plants electricity enters large "step-up" transformers that increase voltage to half a million volts or more.

Electricity flows easily at these large voltages, and travels through high-voltage transmission lines to communities that can be hundreds of miles from the power plants. "Step-down" transformers located at **substations** then reduce the voltage for distribution along street lines. On **utility power poles**, smaller transformers further reduce the voltage to ordinary 120-volt current for household use.

Lines carrying current to the house either run underground, or are strung overhead and attached to a post called a **service head**. Most homes built after 1950 have three wires running to the service head: two power lines, each carrying 120 volts of current, and a grounded neutral wire. Power from the two 120-volt lines may be combined at the **service panel** to supply current to large, 240-volt appliances like clothes dryers or electric water heaters.

Many older homes have only two wires running to the service head, with one 120-volt line and a grounded neutral wire. This older two-wire service is inadequate for today's homes. Contact an electrical contractor and your local power utility company to upgrade to a three-wire service.

Incoming power passes through an **electric meter** that measures power consumption. Power then enters the service panel, where it is distributed to circuits that run throughout the house. The service panel also contains fuses or circuit breakers that shut off power to the individual circuits in the event of a short circuit or an overload. Certain high-wattage appliances, like microwave ovens, are usually plugged into their own individual circuits to prevent overloads.

Voltage ratings determined by power companies and manufacturers have changed over the years. Current rated at 110 volts changed to 115 volts, then 120 volts. Current rated at 220 volts changed to 230 volts, then 240 volts. Similarly, ratings for receptacles, tools, light fixtures, and appliances have changed from 115 volts to 125 volts. These changes will not affect the performance of new devices connected to older wiring. For making electrical calculations, such as the ones shown in "Evaluating Circuits for Safe Capacity" (pages 34 to 35), use a rating of 120 volts or 240 volts for your circuits.

Power plants supply electricity to thousands of homes and businesses. Step-up transformers increase the voltage produced at the plant, making the power flow more easily along high-voltage transmission lines.

Substations are located near the communities they serve. A typical substation takes current from high-voltage transmission lines and reduces it for distribution along street lines.

Utility pole transformers reduce the high-voltage current that flows through power lines along neighborhood streets. A utility pole transformer reduces voltage from 10,000 volts to the normal 120-volt current used in households.

Service head or weather head anchors the service wires and prevents moisture from entering the house.

Service wires supply electricity to the house from the utility company's power lines.

Chandelier

Wall switch

Switch loop

Separate 120-volt circuit for microwave oven.

Receptacles

GFCI receptacles

Electric meter measures the amount of electrical power consumed, and displays the measurement inside a glass dome.

Separate 240-volt circuit for water heater.

Service panel distributes electrical power into circuits.

Grounding rod must be at least 8 feet long and is driven into the ground outside the house.

Grounding wire to metal grounding rod.

Separate 120/240-volt circuit for clothes dryer.

Grounding wire to metal water pipe.

Jumper wire is used to bypass the water meter and ensures an uninterrupted grounding pathway.

Parts of the Electrical System

The service head, sometimes called the weather head, anchors the service wires to the home. Three wires provide the standard 240-volt service necessary for the average home. Older homes may have two-wire service that provides only 120 volts of power. Two-wire service should be upgraded to three-wire service by an electrical contractor.

The electric meter measures the amount of electrical power consumed. It is usually attached to the side of the house, and connects to the service head. A thin metal disc inside the meter rotates when power is used. The electric meter belongs to your local power utility company. If you suspect the meter is not functioning properly, contact the power company.

Grounding wire connects the electrical system to the earth through a cold water pipe and a grounding rod. In the event of an overload or short circuit, the grounding wire allows excess electrical power to find its way harmlessly to the earth.

Light fixtures attach directly to a household electrical system. They are usually controlled with wall switches. The two common types of light fixtures are **incandescent** (page 78) and **fluorescent** (page 88).

The main service panel, sometimes called a fuse box or **breaker box**, distributes power to individual circuits. Fuses or circuit breakers protect each circuit from short circuits and overloads. Fuses and circuit breakers also are used to shut off power to individual circuits while repairs are made.

Electrical boxes enclose wire connections. According to the National Electrical Code, all wire splices or connections must be contained entirely in a plastic or metal electrical box.

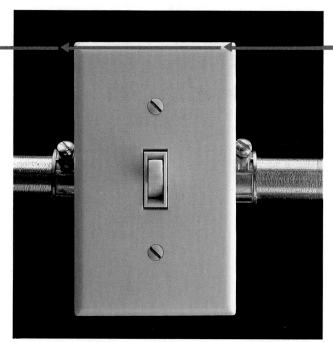

Switches control electrical current passing through hot circuit wires. Switches can be wired to control light fixtures, ceiling fans, appliances, and receptacles.

Receptacles, sometimes called **outlets**, provide plug-in access to electrical power. A 125-volt, 15-amp receptacle with a grounding hole is the most typical receptacle in wiring systems installed after 1965. Most receptacles have two plug-in locations, and are called **duplex receptacles**.

Understanding Circuits

Anatomy of a Circuit

Service panel

Main circuit neutral wire

Circuit breakers

Main circuit hot wires

Grounding wire to metal pipe

An electrical circuit is a continuous loop. Household circuits carry power from the main service panel, throughout the house, and back to the main service panel. Several switches, receptacles, light fixtures, or appliances may be connected to a single circuit.

Current enters a circuit loop on hot wires, and returns along neutral wires. These wires are color coded for easy identification. Hot wires are black or red, and neutral wires are white or light gray. For safety, most circuits include a bare copper or green insulated grounding wire. The grounding wire conducts current in the event of a short circuit or overload, and helps reduce the chance of severe electrical shock. The service panel also has a grounding wire connected to a metal water pipe and metal grounding rod buried underground (pages 16 to 17).

If a circuit carries too much power, it can overload. A fuse or a circuit breaker protects each circuit in case of overloads (pages 28 to 29). To calculate how much power any circuit can carry, see "Evaluating Circuits for Safe Capacity" (pages 34 to 35).

Current returns to the service panel along a neutral circuit wire. Current then becomes part of a main circuit and leaves the house on a large neutral service wire that returns it to the utility pole transformer.

Light switch

Light switch

Circuit wires

White neutral wire

Grounding
wire

Black hot wire

Grounding
screw

Grounding
screw

Light fixture

Receptacle

Receptacle

Grounding
wire

Grounding & Polarization

Service panel

Black hot wire

White neutral wire

Grounding wire

Grounding wire to metal cold water pipe

Normal current flow: Electricity enters an electrical box along a black hot wire, then returns to the service panel along a white neutral wire. Excess current reaches the earth through a grounding wire attached to a metal water pipe and metal grounding rod.

Loose hot wire

Grounding wire

Grounding screw

hort-circuited current: ectricity enters an electrical ox along the black hot wire, en is detoured by a loose wire uching the metal box. The ground- g wire attached to the box picks up this ayward current and channels it safely back to e main service panel. At the service panel the ort-circuited current returns to its source rough a neutral service cable, or reaches the arth through a wire attached to a metal water pe and metal grounding rod. A short circuit so may cause a fuse to blow or a circuit eaker to trip.

Electricity always seeks to return to its source and complete a continuous circuit. In a household wiring system, this return path is provided by white neutral wires that return current to the main service panel. From the service panel, current returns along a neutral service wire to a power pole transformer.

A **grounding wire** provides an additional return path for electrical current. The grounding wire is a safety feature. It is designed to conduct electricity if current seeks to return to the service panel along a path other than the neutral wire, a condition known as a **short circuit.**

A short circuit is a potentially dangerous situation. If an electrical box, tool or appliance becomes short circuited and is touched by a person, the electrical current may attempt to return to its source by passing through that person's body.

However, electrical current always seeks to move along the easiest path. A grounding wire provides a safe, easy path for current to follow back to its source. If a person touches an electrical box, tool, or appliance that has a properly installed grounding wire, any chance of receiving a severe electrical shock is greatly reduced.

In addition, household wiring systems are required to be connected directly to the earth. The earth has a unique ability to absorb the electrons of electrical current. In the event of a short circuit or overload, any excess electricity will find its way along the grounding wire to the earth, where it becomes harmless.

This additional grounding is completed by wiring the household electrical system to a metal cold water pipe and a metal grounding rod that is buried underground.

After 1920, most American homes included receptacles that accepted **polarized plugs.** While not a true grounding method, the two-slot polarized plug and receptacle was designed to keep hot current flowing along black or red wires, and neutral current flowing along white or gray wires.

Armored cable and metal conduit, widely installed in homes during the 1940s, provided a true grounding path. When connected to metal junction boxes, it provided a metal pathway back to the service panel.

Modern cable includes a bare or green insulated copper wire that serves as the grounding path. This grounding wire is connected to all receptacles and metal boxes to provide a continuous pathway for any short-circuited current. A cable with a grounding wire usually is attached to three-slot receptacles. By plugging a three-prong plug into a grounded three-slot receptacle, appliances and tools are protected from short circuits.

Use a receptacle adapter to plug three-prong plugs into two-slot receptacles, but use it only if the receptacle connects to a grounding wire or grounded electrical box. Adapters have short grounding wires or wire loops that attach to the receptacle's coverplate mounting screw. The mounting screw connects the adapter to the grounded metal electrical box.

Modern NM (nonmetallic) cable, found in most wiring systems installed after 1965, contains a bare copper wire that provides grounding for receptacle and switch boxes.

Armored cable, sometimes called BX or Greenfield cable, has a metal sheath that serves as the grounding pathway. Short-circuited current flows through the metal sheath back to the service panel.

Polarized receptacles have a long slot and a short slot. Used with a polarized plug, the polarized receptacle keeps electrical current directed for safety.

Three-slot receptacles are required by code for new homes. They are usually connected to a standard two-wire cable with ground (above, left).

Receptacle adapter allows three-prong plugs to be inserted into two-slot receptacles. The adapter can be used only with grounded receptacles, and the grounding loop or wire of the adapter must be attached to the coverplate mounting screw of the receptacle.

Double-insulated tools have nonconductive plastic bodies to prevent shocks caused by short circuits. Because of these features, double-insulated tools can be used safely with ungrounded receptacles.

Needlenose pliers bends and shapes wires for making screw terminal connections. Some needlenose pliers also have cutting jaws for clipping wires.

Combination tool is essential for home wiring projects. It cuts cables and individual wires, measures wire gauges, and strips the insulation from wires. It has insulated handles.

Continuity tester is used to check switches, lighting fixtures, and other devices for faults. It has a battery that generates current, and a loop of wire for creating an electrical circuit (page 52).

Cordless screwdriver drives a wide variety of screws and fasteners. It is rechargeable, and can be used in either a power or manual mode. A removable tip allows the cordless screwdriver to drive either slotted or Phillips screws.

Neon circuit tester is used to check circuit wires for power. Testing for power is an essential safety step in any electrical repair project (page 70).

Tools for Electrical Repairs

Home electrical repairs require only a few inexpensive tools. As with any tool purchase, invest in quality when buying tools for electrical repairs.

Keep tools clean and dry, and store them securely. Tools with cutting jaws, like needlenose pliers and combination tools, should be resharpened or discarded if the cutting edges become dull.

Several testing tools are used in electrical repair projects. Neon circuit testers (page 70), continuity testers (page 52), and multi-testers (below) should be checked periodically to make sure they are operating properly. Continuity testers and multi-testers have batteries that should be replaced regularly.

Insulated screwdrivers have rubber-coated handles that reduce the risk of shock if the screwdriver should accidentally touch live wires.

Fuse puller is used to remove cartridge-type fuses from the fuse blocks usually found in older main service panels.

Cable ripper fits over NM (nonmetallic) cable. A small cutting point rips the outer plastic vinyl sheath on NM cable so the sheath can be removed without damaging wires.

Multi-tester is a versatile, battery-operated tool frequently used to measure electrical voltages. It also is used to test for continuity in switches, light fixtures, and other electrical devices. An adjustable control makes it possible to measure current ranging from 1 to 1000 volts. A multi-tester is an essential tool for measuring current in low-voltage transformers, like those used to power doorbell and thermostat systems (pages 96 to 109).

Flexible armored cable, sometimes called "Greenfield" or "BX," was used extensively from the 1920s to the 1940s. It was an improvement over knob and tube wiring because it provided a shield for the wires. Armored cable is grounded through the metal coils of the cable itself: there is no separate grounding wire.

Knob and tube wiring, so called because of the shape of its porcelain insulating brackets, was common in wiring systems installed before 1940. Wires are covered with a layer of rubberized cloth fabric called "loom," but have no sheath for additional protection.

Metal conduit protects wires and was installed from the 1940s until 1970. Individual wires are inserted into a rigid tubing. The metal walls of the conduit provide the grounding path: no separate grounding wire is present. Conduit is still recommended by codes for some installations, like exposed wiring in a basement or garage.

Early NM (nonmetallic) cable was used from 1930 until about 1965. It features a flexible rubberized fabric sheathing that protects the individual wires. NM cable greatly simplified wiring installations because separate wires no longer had to be pulled by hand through a metal conduit or armored cable. Early NM cable had no separate grounding wire.

Modern NM (nonmetallic) cable came into use in 1965. It includes a bare copper grounding wire. Wire insulation and outer sheathing are both made of plastic vinyl, which is more durable and moisture-resistant than the rubber materials used in older NM cable. Modern NM cable is inexpensive and easy to install, and is preferred for most installations.

UF (underground feeder) cable has wires that are embedded in a solid-core plastic vinyl sheathing, and includes a bare copper grounding wire. It is designed for installations in damp conditions, such as buried circuits that supply power to a detached garage, shed, or yard light.

Wires & Cables

Wires are made of copper, aluminum, or aluminum covered with a thin layer of copper. Solid copper wires are the best conductors of electricity and are the most widely used. Aluminum and copper-covered aluminum wires require special installation techniques. They are discussed on page 22.

A group of two or more wires enclosed in a metal, rubber, or plastic sheath is called a **cable** (photo, page opposite). The sheath protects the wires from damage. Metal conduit also protects wires, but it is not considered a cable.

Individual wires are covered with rubber or plastic vinyl insulation. An exception is a bare copper grounding wire, which does not need an insulating cover. The insulation is color coded (chart, right) to identify the wire as a hot wire, a neutral wire, or a grounding wire.

In most wiring systems installed after 1965, the wires and cables are insulated with plastic vinyl. This type of insulation is very durable, and can last as long as the house itself.

Before 1965, wires and cables were insulated with rubber. Rubber insulation has a life expectancy of about 25 years (see "Evaluating Old Wiring," pages 122 to 125). Old insulation that is cracked or damaged can be reinforced temporarily by wrapping the wire with plastic electrical tape. However, old wiring with cracked or damaged insulation should be inspected by a qualified electrician to make sure it is safe.

Wires must be large enough for the amperage rating of the circuit (chart, right). A wire that is too small can become dangerously hot. Wire sizes are categorized according to the American Wire Gauge (AWG) system. To check the size of a wire, use the wire stripper openings of a combination tool (page 18) as a guide.

Everything You Need:

Tools: cable ripper, combination tool, screwdriver, needlenose pliers.

Materials: wire nuts, pigtail wires (if needed).

See Inspector's Notebook:

- Common Cable Problems (pages 112 to 113).
- Checking Wire Connections (pages 114 to 115).
- Electrical Box Inspection (pages 116 to 117).

Wire Color Chart

Wire color	Function
White	Neutral wire carrying current at zero voltage.
Black	Hot wire carrying current at full voltage .
Red	Hot wire carrying current at full voltage .
White, black markings	Hot wire carrying current at full voltage .
Green	Serves as a grounding pathway.
Bare copper	Serves as a grounding pathway.

Individual wires are color coded to identify their function. In some circuit installations, the white wire serves as a hot wire that carries voltage. If so, this white wire may be labeled with black tape or paint to identify it as a hot wire.

Wire Size Chart

Wire gauge	Wire capacity & use
#6	60 amps, 240 volts; central air conditioner, electric furnace.
#8	40 amps, 240 volts; electric range, central air conditioner.
#10	30 amps, 240 volts; window air conditioner, clothes dryer.
#12	20 amps, 120 volts; light fixtures, receptacles, microwave oven.
#14	15 amps, 120 volts; light fixtures, receptacles.
#16	Light-duty extension cords.
#18 to 22	Thermostats, doorbells, security systems.

Wire sizes (shown actual size) are categorized by the American Wire Gauge system. The larger the wire size, the smaller the AWG number.

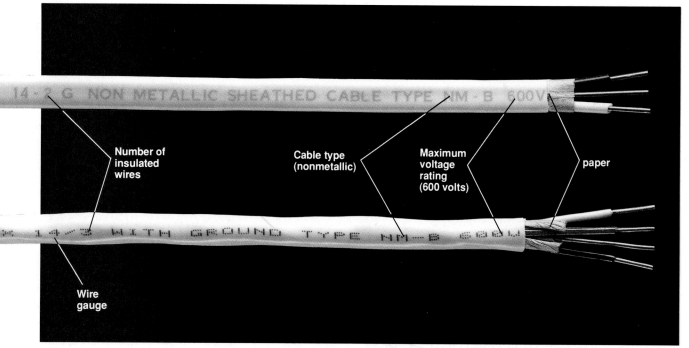

NM (nonmetallic) cable is labeled with the number of insulated wires it contains. The bare grounding wire is not counted. For example, a cable marked 14/2 G (or 14/2 WITH GROUND) contains two insulated 14-gauge wires, plus a bare copper grounding wire.

Cable marked 14/3 WITH GROUND has three 14-gauge wires plus a grounding wire. A strip of paper inside the cable protects the individual wires. NM cable also is stamped with a maximum voltage rating, as determined by Underwriters Laboratories (UL).

Aluminum Wire

Inexpensive aluminum wire was used in place of copper in many wiring systems installed during the late 1960s and early 1970s, when copper prices were high. Aluminum wire is identified by its silver color,

and by the AL stamp on the cable sheathing. A variation, copper-clad aluminum wire, has a thin coating of copper bonded to a solid aluminum core.

By the early 1970s, all-aluminum wire was found to pose a safety hazard if connected to a switch or receptacle with brass or copper screw terminals. Because aluminum expands and contracts at a different rate than copper or brass, the wire connections could become loose. In some instances, fires resulted.

Existing aluminum wiring in homes is considered safe if proper installation methods have been followed, and if the wires are connected to special switches and receptacles designed to be used with aluminum wire. If you have aluminum wire in your home, have a qualified electrical inspector review the system. Copper-coated aluminum wire is not a hazard.

For a short while, switches and receptacles with an Underwriters Laboratories (UL) wire compatibility

rating of AL-CU were used with both aluminum and copper wiring. However, these devices proved to be hazardous when connected to aluminum wire. AL-CU devices should not be used with aluminum wiring.

In 1971, switches and receptacles designed for use with aluminum wiring were introduced. They are marked CO/ALR. This mark is now the only approved rating for aluminum wires. If your home has aluminum wires connected to a switch or receptacle without a CO/ALR rating stamp, replace the device with a switch or receptacle rated CO/ALR.

A switch or receptacle that has no wire compatibility rating printed on the mounting strap or casing should not be used with aluminum wires. These devices are designed for use with copper wires only.

How to Strip NM (Nonmetallic) Cable & Wires

1 Measure and mark the cable 8" to 10" from end. Slide the cable ripper onto the cable, and squeeze tool firmly to force cutting point through plastic sheathing.

2 Grip the cable tightly with one hand, and pull the cable ripper toward the end of the cable to cut open the plastic sheathing.

3 Peel back the plastic sheathing and the paper wrapping from the individual wires.

4 Cut away the excess plastic sheathing and paper wrapping, using the cutting jaws of a combination tool.

5 Cut the individual wires, if necessary, using the cutting jaws of the combination tool.

6 Strip insulation from each wire, using the stripper openings. Choose the opening that matches the gauge of the wire, and take care not to nick or scratch the ends of the wires.

How to Connect Wires to Screw Terminals

1 Strip about ¾" of insulation from each wire, using a combination tool. Choose the stripper opening that matches the gauge of the wire, then clamp wire in tool. Pull the wire firmly to remove plastic insulation.

2 Form a C-shaped loop in the end of each wire, using a needle-nose pliers. The wire should have no scratches or nicks.

3 Hook each wire around the screw terminal so it forms a clockwise loop. Tighten screw firmly. Insulation should just touch head of screw. Never place the ends of two wires under a single screw terminal. Instead, use a pigtail wire (page opposite).

How to Connect Wires with Push-in Fittings

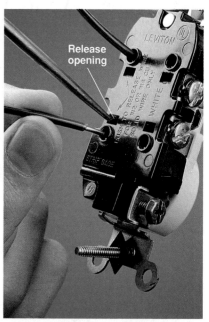

1 Mark the amount of insulation to be stripped from each wire, using the strip gauge on the back of the switch or receptacle. Strip the wires using a combination tool (step 1, above). Never use push-in fittings with aluminum wiring.

2 Insert the bare copper wires firmly into the push-in fittings on the back of the switch or receptacle. When inserted, wires should have no bare copper exposed.

Remove a wire from a push-in fitting by inserting a small nail or screwdriver in the release opening next to the wire. Wire will pull out easily.

How to Connect Two or More Wires with a Wire Nut

1 Strip about ½" of insulation from each wire. Hold the wires parallel, and twist them together in a clockwise direction, using a needle-nose pliers or combination tool.

2 Screw the wire nut onto the twisted wires. Tug gently on each wire to make sure it is secure. In a proper connection, no bare wire should be exposed past the bottom of the wire nut.

Wire nut (shown in cutaway) has metal threads that grip the bare ends of the wires. When connected, the wire nut should completely cover the bare wires.

How to Pigtail Two or More Wires

 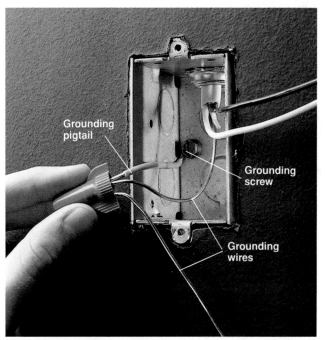

Connect two or more wires to a single screw terminal with a pigtail. A pigtail is a short piece of wire. One end of the pigtail connects to a screw terminal, and the other end connects to circuit wires, using a wire nut. A pigtail also can be used to lengthen circuit wires that are too short (page 116).

Grounding pigtail has green insulation, and is available with a preattached grounding screw. This grounding screw connects to the grounded metal electrical box. The end of the pigtail wire connects to the bare copper grounding wires with a wire nut.

Service Panels

Every home has a main service panel that distributes electrical current to the individual circuits. The main service panel usually is found in the basement, garage, or utility area, and can be identified by its metal casing. Before making any repair to your electrical system, you must shut off power to the correct circuit at the main service panel. The service panel should be indexed (pages 30 to 33) so circuits can be identified easily.

Service panels vary in appearance, depending on the age of the system. Very old wiring may operate on 30-amp service that has only two circuits. New homes can have 200-amp service with 30 or more circuits. Find the size of the service by reading the amperage rating printed on the main fuse block or main circuit breaker.

Regardless of age, all service panels have **fuses** or **circuit breakers** (pages 28 to 29) that control each circuit and protect them from overloads. In general, older service panels use fuses, while newer service panels use circuit breakers.

In addition to the main service panel, your electrical system may have a subpanel that controls some of the circuits in the home. A subpanel has its own circuit breakers or fuses, and is installed to control circuits that have been added to an existing wiring system.

The subpanel resembles the main service panel, but is usually smaller. It may be located near the main panel, or it may be found near the areas served by the new circuits. Garages and attics that have been updated often have their own subpanels. If your home has a subpanel, make sure that its circuits are indexed correctly.

When handling fuses or circuit breakers, make sure the area around the service panel is dry. Never remove the protective cover on the service panel. After turning off a circuit to make electrical repairs, remember to always test the circuit for power before touching any wires.

Metal contacts

Knife-blade switch lever

Plug fuses

A 30-amp service panel, common in systems installed before 1950, is identified by a ceramic fuse holder containing two plug fuses and a "knife-blade" switch lever. The fuse holder sometimes is contained in a black metal box mounted in an entryway or basement. This 30-amp service panel provides only 120 volts of power, and now is considered inadequate. For example, most home loan programs, like the FHA (Federal Housing Administration), require that 30-amp service be updated to 100 amps or more before a home can qualify for mortgage financing.

To shut off power to individual circuits in a 30-amp panel, carefully unscrew the plug fuses, touching only the insulated rim of the fuse. To shut off power to the entire house, open the knife-blade switch. Be careful not to touch the metal contacts on the switch.

A 60-amp fuse panel often is found in wiring systems installed between 1950 and 1965. It usually is housed in a gray metal cabinet that contains four individual plug fuses, plus one or two pull-out fuse blocks that hold cartridge fuses. This type of panel is regarded as adequate for a small, 1100-square-foot house that has no more than one 240-volt appliance. Many homeowners update 60-amp service to 100 amps or more so that additional lighting and appliance circuits can be added to the system. Home loan programs also may require that 60-amp service be updated before a home can qualify for financing.

To shut off power to a circuit, carefully unscrew the plug fuse, touching only its insulated rim. To shut off power to the entire house, hold the handle of the main fuse block and pull sharply to remove it. Major appliance circuits are controlled with another cartridge fuse block. Shut off the appliance circuit by pulling out this fuse block.

A circuit breaker panel providing 100 amps or more of power is common in wiring systems installed during the 1960s and later. A circuit breaker panel is housed in a gray metal cabinet that contains two rows of individual circuit breakers. The size of the service can be identified by reading the amperage rating of the main circuit breaker, which is located at the top of the main service panel.

A 100-amp service panel is now the minimum standard for most new housing. It is considered adequate for a medium-sized house with no more than three major electric appliances. However, larger houses with more electrical appliances require a service panel that provides 150 amps or more.

To shut off power to individual circuits in a circuit breaker panel, flip the lever on the appropriate circuit breaker to the OFF position. To shut off the power to the entire house, turn the main circuit breaker to the OFF position.

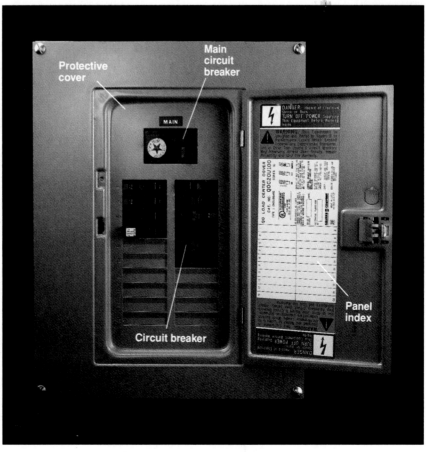

Fuses & Circuit Breakers

Cartridge fuses

Time-delay fuses

Fast acting fuse

Regular plug fuse

Time-delay fuses

Regular plug fuse

Tamper-proof fuses

Regular plug fuse

Fuses are used in older service panels. Plug fuses usually control 120-volt circuits rated for 15, 20 or 30 amps. Tamper-proof plug fuses have threads that fit only matching sockets, making it impossible to install a wrong-sized fuse. Time-delay fuses absorb temporary heavy power load without blowing. Cartridge fuses control 240-volt circuits and range from 30 to 100 amps.

GFCI circuit breaker

20-amp single-pole (120-volt)

40-amp, single-pole (120-volt)

40-amp double-pole (240-volt)

15-amp, single-pole (120-volt)

Circuit breakers are used in newer service panels. Single-pole breakers rated for 15 or 20 amps control 120-volt circuits. Double-pole breakers rated for 20 to 50 amps control 240-volt circuits. GFCI (ground-fault circuit-interrupter) breakers provide shock protection for the entire circuit.

Fuses and circuit breakers are safety devices designed to protect the electrical system from short circuits and overloads. Fuses and circuit breakers are located in the main service panel.

Most service panels installed before 1965 rely on fuses to control and protect individual circuits. Screw-in plug fuses protect 120-volt circuits that power lights and receptacles. Cartridge fuses protect 240-volt appliance circuits and the main shutoff of the service panel.

Inside each fuse is a current-carrying metal alloy ribbon. If a circuit is overloaded (pages 34 to 35), the metal ribbon melts and stops the flow of power. A fuse must match the amperage rating of the circuit. Never replace a fuse with one that has a larger amperage rating.

In most service panels installed after 1965, circuit breakers protect and control individual circuits. Single-pole circuit breakers protect 120-volt circuits, and double-pole circuit breakers protect 240-volt circuits. Amperage ratings for circuit breakers range from 15 to 100 amps.

Each circuit breaker has a permanent metal strip that heats up and bends when voltage passes through it. If a circuit is overloaded, the metal strip inside the breaker bends enough to "trip" the switch and stop the flow of power. If a circuit breaker trips frequently even though the power demand is small, the mechanism inside the breaker may be worn out. Worn circuit breakers should be replaced by an electrician.

When a fuse blows or a circuit breaker trips, it is usually because there are too many light fixtures and plug-in appliances drawing power through the circuit. Move some of the plug-in appliances to another circuit, then replace the fuse or reset the breaker. If the fuse blows or breaker trips again immediately, there may be a short circuit in the system. Call a licensed electrician if you suspect a short circuit.

Everything You Need:

Tools: fuse puller (for cartridge fuses only).

Materials: replacement fuse.

How to Identify & Replace a Blown Plug Fuse

1 Go to the main service panel and locate the blown fuse. If the metal ribbon inside fuse is cleanly melted (right), the circuit was overloaded. If window in fuse is discolored (left), there was a short circuit in the system.

2 Unscrew the fuse, being careful to touch only the insulated rim of the fuse. Replace it with a fuse that has the same amperage rating.

How to Remove, Test & Replace a Cartridge Fuse

1 Remove cartridge fuses by gripping the handle of the fuse block and pulling sharply.

2 Remove the individual cartridge fuses from the block, using a fuse puller.

3 Test each fuse, using a continuity tester. If the tester glows, the fuse is good. If the tester does not glow, replace the fuse with one that has the same amperage rating.

How to Reset a Circuit Breaker

1 Open the service panel and locate the tripped breaker. The lever on the tripped breaker will be either in the OFF position, or in a position between ON and OFF.

2 Reset the tripped circuit breaker by pressing the circuit breaker lever all the way to the OFF position, then pressing it to the ON position.

Test GFCI circuit breakers by pushing TEST button. Breaker should trip to the OFF position. If not, the breaker is faulty and must be replaced by an electrician.

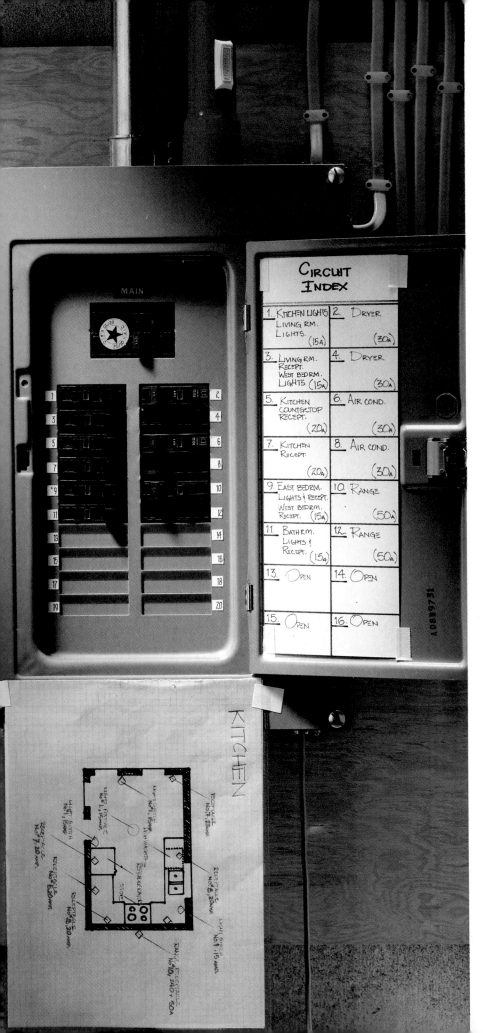

CIRCUIT INDEX

1. KITCHEN LIGHTS LIVING RM. LIGHTS. (15A)	2. DRYER (30A)
3. LIVING RM. RECEPT. WEST BEDRM. LIGHTS (15A)	4. DRYER (30A)
5. KITCHEN COUNTERTOP RECEPT. (20A)	6. AIR COND. (30A)
7. KITCHEN RECEPT. (20A)	8. AIR COND. (30A)
9. EAST BEDRM. LIGHTS + RECEPT. WEST BEDRM. RECEPT. (15A)	10. RANGE (50A)
11. BATH RM. LIGHTS + RECEPT. (15A)	12. RANGE (50A)
13. OPEN	14. OPEN
15. OPEN	16. OPEN

Mapping Circuits & Indexing the Service Panel

Making repairs to an electrical system is easier and safer if you have an accurate, up-to-date map of your home's electrical circuits. A circuit map shows all lights, appliances, switches, and receptacles connected to each circuit. The map allows you to index the main service panel so that the correct circuit can be shut off when repairs are needed.

Mapping all the circuits and indexing the main service panel requires four to six hours. If your service panel was indexed by a previous owner, it is a good idea to make your own circuit map to make sure the old index is accurate. If circuits have been added or changed, the old index will be outdated.

The easiest way to map circuits is to turn on one circuit at a time and check to see which light fixtures, receptacles, and appliances are powered by the circuit. All electrical devices must be in good working condition before you begin.

A circuit map also will help you evaluate the electrical demands on each circuit (pages 34 to 35). This information can help you determine if your wiring system needs to be updated.

Everything You Need:

Tools: pens, circuit tester.

Materials: graph paper, masking tape.

See Inspector's Notebook:

• Service Panel Inspection (page 111).

How to Map Circuits & Index a Service Panel

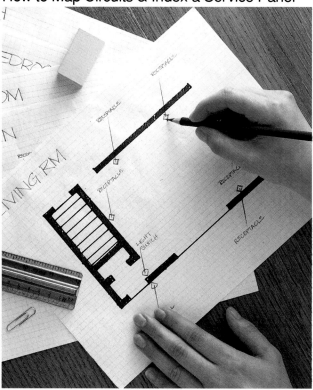

1 Make a sketch of each room in the house on graph paper. Include the hallways, basement and attic, and all utility areas. Or, use a blueprint of your house.

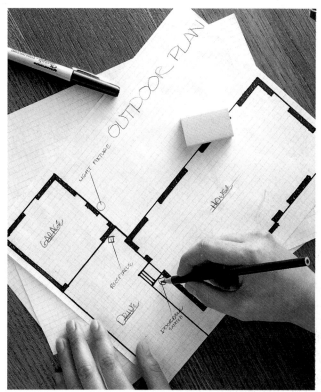

2 Make a sketch of the outside of the house, the garage, and any other separate structures that are wired for electricity.

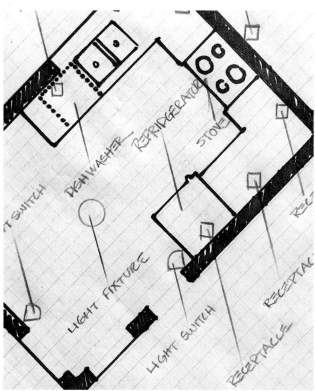

3 On each sketch, indicate the location of all receptacles, light fixtures, switches, appliances, doorbells, thermostats, heaters, fans, and air conditioners.

4 At the main service panel, number each circuit breaker or fuse. Turn off all the circuit breakers or loosen all the fuses, but leave the main shutoff in the ON position.

(continued next page)

5 Turn on one circuit at a time by flipping the circuit breaker lever or tightening the correct fuse. Note the amperage rating printed on the circuit breaker lever, or on the rim of the fuse (page 28).

6 Turn on switches, lights, and appliances throughout the house, and identify those that are powered by the circuit. Write the circuit number and amperage rating on a piece of masking tape. The tape makes a handy temporary reference.

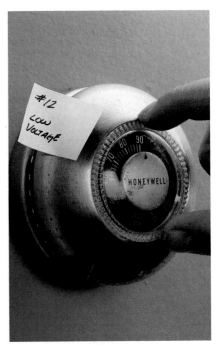

7 Test receptacles for power, using a neon circuit tester. Make sure to check both halves of the receptacle.

8 Indicate which circuit supplies power to each receptacle. Although uncommon, remember that receptacles can be wired so that each half of the receptacle is powered by a different circuit.

9 To check the furnace for power, set thermostat to highest temperature setting. Furnaces and their low-voltage thermostats are on the same circuit. If the circuit is hot, the furnace will begin running. The lowest temperature setting will turn on central air conditioner.

10 Check electric water heater for power by setting its thermostat to highest temperature setting. Water heater will begin to heat if it is powered by the circuit.

11 Check the doorbell system for power by ringing all of the doorbells.

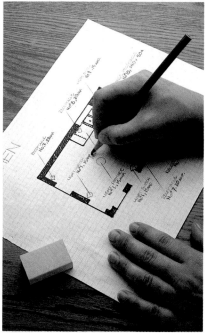

12 On the circuit maps, indicate the circuit number, the voltage, and the amperage rating of each receptacle, switch, light fixture, and appliance.

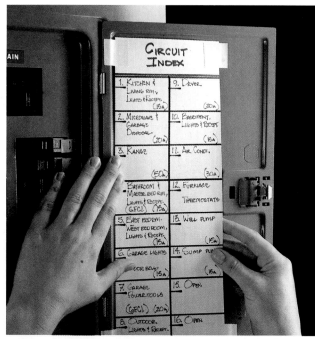

13 On the door of the main service panel, tape an index that provides a brief summary of all the fixtures, receptacles, and appliances that are powered by each circuit.

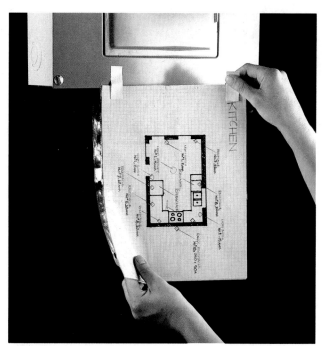

14 Attach the completed circuit maps to the main service panel, and make sure the power is turned on for all the circuits.

Evaluating Circuits for Safe Capacity

Every electrical circuit in a home has a "safe capacity." Safe capacity is the total amount of power the circuit wires can carry without tripping circuit breakers or blowing fuses. According to the National Electrical Code, the power used by light fixtures, lamps, tools, and appliances, called the "demand," must not exceed the safe capacity of the circuit.

Finding the safe capacity and the demand of a circuit is easy. Make these simple calculations to reduce the chances of tripped circuit breakers or blown fuses, or to help plan the location of new appliances or plug-in lamps.

First, determine the amperage and voltage rating of the circuit. If you have an up-to-date circuit map (pages 30 to 33) these ratings should be indicated on the map. If not, open the service panel door and read the amperage rating printed on the circuit breaker, or on the rim of the fuse. The type of circuit breaker or fuse (page 28) indicates the voltage of the circuit.

Use the amperage and voltage ratings to find the safe capacity of the circuit. Safe capacities of the most common household circuits are given in the table at right.

Safe capacities can be calculated by multiplying the amperage rating by voltage. The answer is the total capacity, expressed in **watts**, a unit of electrical measurement. To find the safe capacity, reduce the total capacity by 20%.

Next, compare the safe capacity of the circuit to the total power demand. To find the demand, add the wattage ratings for all light fixtures, lamps, and appliances on the circuit. For lights, use the wattage rating printed on the light bulbs. Wattage ratings for appliances often are printed on the manufacturer's label. Approximate wattage ratings for many common household items are given in the table on the opposite page. If you are unsure about the wattage rating of a tool or appliance, use the highest number shown in the table to make calculations.

Compare the power demand to the safe capacity. The power demand should not exceed the safe capacity of the circuit. If it does, you must move lamps or appliances to another circuit. Or, make sure that the power demand of the lamps and appliances turned on **at the same time** does not exceed the safe capacity of the circuit.

Amps x Volts	Total Capacity	Safe Capacity
15 A x 120 V =	1800 watts	1440 watts
20 A x 120 V =	2400 watts	1920 watts
25 A x 120 V =	3000 watts	2400 watts
30 A x 120 V =	3600 watts	2880 watts
20 A x 240 V =	4800 watts	3840 watts
30 A x 240 V =	7200 watts	5760 watts

How to Find Wattage & Amperage Ratings

Light bulb wattage ratings are printed on the top of the bulb. If a light fixture has more than one bulb, remember to add the wattages of all the bulbs to find the total wattage of the fixture.

Appliance wattage ratings are often listed on the manufacturer's label. Or, use table of typical wattage ratings on the opposite page.

Amperage rating can be used to find the wattage of an appliance. Multiply the amperage by the voltage of the circuit. For example, a 13-amp, 120-volt circular saw is rated for 1560 watts.

Sample Circuit Evaluation

Circuit # _6_ Amps _20_ Volts _120_ Total capacity _2400_ (watts) Safe capacity _1920_ (watts)

Appliance or fixture	Notes	Wattage rating
Refrigerator	Constant use	480
Ceiling light	3 - 60 watt bulbs	180
Microwave oven		625
Electric can opener	Occasional use	144
Stereo	Portable boom box	300
Ceiling light (hallway)	2 60 watt bulbs	120
	Total demand:	1849 (watts)

Photocopy this sample circuit evaluation to keep a record of the power demand of each circuit. The words and numbers printed in blue will not reproduce on photocopies. In this sample kitchen circuit, the demand on the circuit is very close to the safe capacity. Adding another appliance, such as an electric frying pan, could overload the circuit and cause a fuse to blow or a circuit breaker to trip.

Typical Wattage Ratings (120-volt Circuit Except Where Noted)

Appliance	Amps	Watts	Appliance	Amps	Watts
Air conditioner (central)	21 (240-v)	5040	Hair dryer	5 to 10	600 to 1200
Air conditioner (window)	6 to 13	720 to 1560	Heater (portable)	7 to 12	840 to 1440
Blender	2 to 4	240 to 480	Microwave oven	4 to 7	480 to 840
Broiler	12.5	1500	Range (oven/stove)	16 to 32 (240-v)	3840 to 7680
Can opener	1.2	144	Refrigerator	2 to 4	240 to 480
Circular saw	10 to 12	1200 to 1440	Router	8	960
Coffee maker	4 to 8	480 to 960	Sander (portable)	2 to 5	240 to 600
Clothes dryer	16.5 to 34 (240-v)	3960 to 8160	Saw (table)	7 to 10	840 to 1200
Clothes iron	9	1080	Sewing machine	1	120
Computer	4 to 7	480 to 840	Stereo	2.5 to 4	300 to 480
Dishwasher	8.5 to 12.5	1020 to 1500	Television (b & w)	2	240
Drill (portable)	2 to 4	240 to 480	Television (color)	2.5	300
Fan (ceiling)	3.5	420	Toaster	9	1080
Fan (portable)	2	240	Trash compactor	4 to 8	480 to 960
Freezer	2 to 4	240 to 480	Vacuum cleaner	6 to 11	720 to 1320
Frying pan	9	1080	Waffle iron	7.5	900
Furnace, forced-air gas	6.5 to 13	780 to 1560	Washing machine	12.5	1500
Garbage disposer	3.5 to 7.5	420 to 900	Water heater	10.5 to 21 (240-v)	2520 to 5040

Octagonal box, Grounding screw, Grounding wires, Coverplate, Hot wires, Knockouts, Metal brace, NM (nonmetallic) cable, Cable clamp, Neutral wires, Wire nut

Octagonal boxes usually contain wire connections for ceiling fixtures. Cables are inserted into the box through knockout openings, and are held with cable clamps. Because the ceiling fixture attaches directly to the box, the box should be anchored firmly to a framing member. Often, it is nailed directly to a ceiling joist. However, metal braces are available that allow a box to be mounted between joists or studs. A properly installed octagonal box can support a ceiling fixture weighing up to 35 pounds. Any box must be covered with a tightly fitting coverplate, and the box must not have open knockouts.

Electrical Boxes

The National Electrical Code requires that wire connections or cable splices be contained inside an approved metal or plastic box. This shields framing members and other flammable materials from electrical sparks. If you have exposed wire connections or cable splices, protect your home by installing electrical boxes.

Electrical boxes come in several shapes. Rectangular and square boxes are used for switches and receptacles. Rectangular (2" × 3") boxes are used for single switches or duplex receptacles. Square (4" × 4") boxes are used anytime it is convenient for two switches or receptacles to be wired or "ganged" in one box, an arrangement common in kitchens or entry hallways. Octagonal electrical boxes contain wire connections for ceiling fixtures.

All electrical boxes are available in different depths. A box must be deep enough so a switch or receptacle can be removed or installed easily without crimping and damaging the circuit wires. Replace an undersized box with a larger box, using the Electrical Box Chart (right) as a guide. The NEC also says that all electrical boxes must remain accessible. Never cover an electrical box with drywall, paneling, or wallcoverings.

See Inspector's Notebook:

- Electrical Box Inspection (pages 116 to 117).
- Common Cable Problems (pages 112 to 113).

Electrical Box Chart

Box Shape		Maximum number of individual wires in box*	
		14-gauge	12-gauge
2"×3" rectangular	2½" deep	3	3
	3½" deep	5	4
4"×4" square	1½" deep	6	5
	2⅛" deep	9	7
Octagonal	1½" deep	4	3
	2⅛" deep	7	6

* Do not count pigtail wires or grounding wires.

Common Electrical Boxes

Rectangular boxes are used with wall switches and duplex receptacles. Single-size rectangular boxes (shown above) may have detachable sides that allow them to be ganged together to form double-size boxes.

Square 4" × 4" boxes are large enough for most wiring applications. They are used for cable splices and ganged receptacles or switches. To install one switch or receptacle in a square box, use an adapter cover.

Braced octagonal boxes fit between ceiling joists. The metal braces extend to fit any joist spacing, and are nailed or screwed to framing members.

Outdoor boxes have sealed seams and foam gaskets to guard a switch or receptacle against moisture. Corrosion-resistant coatings protect all metal parts.

Retrofit boxes upgrade older boxes to larger sizes. One type (above) has built-in clamps that tighten against the inside of a wall and hold the box in place. A retrofit box with flexible brackets is shown on pages 40 to 41.

Plastic boxes are common in new construction. They can be used only with NM (nonmetallic) cable. Box may include preattached nails for anchoring the box to framing members.

Electrical boxes are required for all wire connections. The box protects wood and other flammable materials from electrical sparks (arcing). Electrical boxes should always be anchored to joists or studs.

Installing an Electrical Box

Install an electrical box any time you find exposed wire connections or cable splices. Exposed connections sometimes can be found in older homes, where wires attach to light fixtures. Exposed splices (page 113) can be found in areas where NM (nonmetallic) cable runs through uncovered joists or wall studs, such as in an unfinished basement or utility room.

When installing an electrical box, make sure there is enough cable to provide about 8" of wire inside the box. If the wires are too short, you can add pigtails to lengthen them (page 116). If the electrical box is metal, make sure the circuit grounding wires are pigtailed to the box.

Everything You Need:

Tools: neon circuit tester, screwdriver, hammer, combination tool.

Materials: screws or nails, electrical box, cable connectors, pigtail wire, wire nuts.

How to Install an Electrical Box for Cable Splices

1 Turn off power to circuit wires at the main service panel. Carefully remove any tape or wire nuts from the exposed splice. Avoid contact with the bare wire ends until the wires have been tested for power.

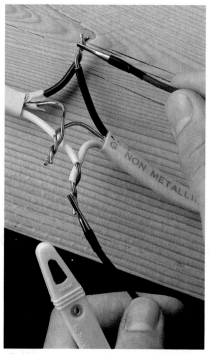

2 Test for power. Touch one probe of a circuit tester to the black hot wires, and touch other probe to the white neutral wires. The tester should not glow. If it does, the wires are still hot. Shut off power to correct circuit at the main service panel. Disconnect the splice wires.

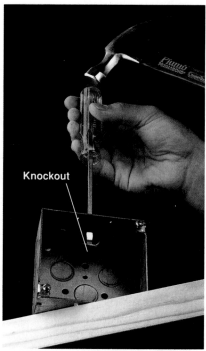

Knockout

3 Open one knockout for each cable that will enter the box, using a hammer and screwdriver. Any unopened knockouts should remain sealed.

4 Anchor the electrical box to a wooden framing member, using screws or nails.

Cable clamp

Cable sheathing

5 Thread each cable through a cable clamp. Tighten the clamp with a screwdriver. Do not over-tighten. Overtightening can damage cable sheathing.

Locknut

6 Insert the cables into the electri-cal box, and screw a locknut onto each cable clamp.

Locknut

Lugs

7 Tighten the locknuts by pushing against the lugs with the blade of a screwdriver.

Grounding screw

8 Use wire nuts to reconnect the wires. Pigtail the copper ground-ing wires to the green grounding screw in the back of the box.

Coverplate

9 Carefully tuck the wires into the box, and attach the coverplate. Turn on the power to the circuit at the main service panel. Make sure the box remains accessible, and is not covered with finished walls or ceilings.

Replacing an Electrical Box

Replace any electrical box that is too small for the number of wires it contains. Forcing wires into an undersized box can damage wires, disturb wire connections, and create a potential fire hazard.

Boxes that are too small often are found when repairing or replacing switches, receptacles, or light fixtures. If you find a box so small that you have difficulty fitting the wires inside, replace it with a larger box. Use the chart on page 36 as a guide when choosing a replacement box.

Metal and plastic retrofit electrical boxes are available in a variety of styles, and can be purchased at any hardware store or home center. Most can be installed without damaging the wall surfaces.

Everything You Need:

Tools: screwdriver, neon circuit tester, reciprocating saw, hammer, needlenose pliers.

Materials: electrical tape, retrofit electrical box with flexible brackets, grounding screw.

How to Replace an Electrical Box

1 Shut off the power to the circuit at the main service panel. Test for power with a neon circuit tester (switches, page 57; receptacles, page 70; light fixtures, page 80). Disconnect and remove receptacle, switch, or fixture from the existing box.

2 Examine the box to determine how it was installed. Most older metal boxes are attached to framing members with nails, and the nail heads will be visible inside the box.

3 Cut through the mounting nails by slipping the metal-cutting blade of a reciprocating saw between the box and framing member. Take care not to damage the circuit wires. Disconnect wires.

If box is mounted with straps (shown with wall cut away) remove the box by cutting through the straps, using a reciprocating saw and metal-cutting blade. Take care not to damage the wires.

4 To prevent wires from falling into wall cavity, gather wires from each cable and tie them together, using pieces of string.

5 Secure the string to the wires, using a piece of plastic electrical tape.

6 Disconnect the internal clamps or locknuts that hold the circuit cables to the box.

Locknuts

7 Pull old electrical box from wall. Take care not to damage insulation on circuit wires, and hold on to string to make sure wires do not fall inside wall cavity.

8 Tape the wires to the edge of the wall cutout.

9 Punch out one knockout for each cable that will enter the new electrical box, using a screwdriver and hammer.

10 Thread cables into the new electrical box, and slide the box into the wall opening. Tighten the internal clamps or locknuts holding the circuit cables to the electrical box. Remove the strings.

Bracket arms

Inside tab

11 Insert flexible brackets into the wall on each side of the electrical box. Pull out bracket arms until inside tab is tight against inside of the wall.

Bracket arms

12 Bend bracket arms around walls of box, using needle-nose pliers. Reinstall the fixture, and turn on the power to the circuit at the main service panel.

Rotary snap switches are found in many installations completed between 1900 and 1920. Handle is twisted clockwise to turn light on and off. The switch is enclosed in a ceramic housing.

Push-button switches were widely used from 1920 until about 1940. Many switches of this type are still in operation. Reproductions of this switch type are available for restoration projects.

Toggle switches were introduced in the 1930s. This early design has a switch mechanism that is mounted in a ceramic housing sealed with a layer of insulating paper.

Common Wall-switch Problems

An average wall switch is turned on and off more than 1,000 times each year. Because switches receive constant use, wire connections can loosen and switch parts gradually wear out. If a switch no longer operates smoothly, it must be repaired or replaced.

The methods for repairing or replacing a switch vary slightly, depending on the switch type and its location along an electrical circuit. When working on a switch, use the photographs on pages 44 to 51 to identify your switch type and its wiring configuration. Individual switch styles may vary from manufacturer to manufacturer, but the basic switch types are universal.

It is possible to replace most ordinary wall switches with a specialty switch, like a timer switch or an electronic switch. When installing a specialty switch (pages 49 to 51), make sure it is compatible with the wiring configuration of the switch box.

See Inspector's Notebook:
• Common Cable Problems (pages 112 to 113).
• Checking Wire Connections (pages 114 to 115).
• Inspecting Switches (page 121).

Metal arm

Screw terminals

Hot wire

Typical wall switch has a movable metal arm that opens and closes the electrical circuit. When the switch is ON, the arm completes the circuit and power flows between the screw terminals and through the black hot wire to the light fixture. When the switch is OFF, the arm lifts away to interrupt the circuit, and no power flows. Switch problems can occur if the screw terminals are not tight, or if the metal arm inside the switch wears out.

Toggle switches were improved during the 1950s, and are now the most commonly used type. This switch type was the first to use a sealed plastic housing that protects the inner switch mechanism from dust and moisture.

Mercury switches became common in the early 1960s. They conduct electrical current by means of a sealed vial of mercury. Although more expensive than other types, mercury switches are durable: some are guaranteed for 50 years.

Electronic motion-sensor switch has an infrared eye that senses movement and automatically turns on lights when a person enters a room. Motion-sensor switches can provide added security against intruders.

Problem	Repair
Fuse burns out or circuit breaker trips when the switch is turned on.	1. Tighten any loose wire connections on switch (pages 56 to 57). 2. Move lamps or plug-in appliances to other circuits to prevent overloads (page 34). 3. Test switch (pages 52 to 55), and replace, if needed (pages 56 to 59). 4. Repair or replace faulty fixture (pages 78 to 93) or faulty appliance.
Light fixture or permanently installed appliance does not work.	1. Replace burned-out light bulb. 2. Check for blown fuse or tripped circuit breaker to make sure circuit is operating (pages 28 to 29). 3. Check for loose wire connections on switch (pages 56 to 57). 4. Test switch (pages 52 to 55), and replace, if needed (pages 56 to 59). 5. Repair or replace light fixture (pages 78 to 93) or appliance.
Light fixture flickers.	1. Tighten light bulb in the socket. 2. Check for loose wire connections on switch (pages 56 to 57). 3. Repair or replace light fixture (pages 78 to 93), or switch (pages 56 to 59).
Switch buzzes or is warm to the touch.	1. Check for loose wire connections on switch (pages 56 to 57). 2. Test switch (pages 52 to 55), and replace, if needed (pages 56 to 59). 3. Move lamps or appliances to other circuits to reduce demand (page 34).
Switch lever does not stay in position.	Replace worn-out switch (pages 56 to 59).

Wall-switch Basics

Wire compatibility rating

NOTE: Position of the screw terminals on switch may vary, depending on manufacturer

CU AND CU-CLAD WIRE ONLY

MADE IN U.S.A.

LEVITON

Screw terminals

15A. 120 VAC ONLY

UND LAB INC LIST

Underwriters Laboratories (UL) approval

Amperage & voltage ratings

Front

Mounting screw

Wire gauge rating

#12 & #14 SOLID CU. WIRE ONLY

PUSH TO RELEASE

Push-in fittings

STRIP GAGE

FOR BACK WIRING ONLY

Wire strip gauge

PUSH TO RELEASE

Wire release opening for push-in fittings

#12 & #14 SOLID CU. WIRE ONLY

Mounting strap

Back

Wall switches are available in three general types. To repair or replace a switch, it is important to identify its type.

Single-pole switches are used to control a set of lights from one location. **Three-way switches** are used to control a set of lights from two different locations, and are always installed in pairs. **Four-way switches** are used in combination with a pair of three-way switches to control a set of lights from three or more locations.

Identify switch types by counting the screw terminals. Single-pole switches have two screw terminals, three-way switches have three screw terminals, and four-way switches have four.

Some switches may include a grounding screw terminal, which is identified by its green color. Although grounded switches are not required by most electrical codes, some electricians recommend they be used in bathrooms, kitchens, and basements. When pigtailed to the grounding wires, the grounding screw provides added protection against shock.

When replacing a switch, choose a new switch that has the same number of screw terminals as the old one. The location of the screws on the switch body varies, depending on the manufacturer, but these differences will not affect the switch operation.

Newer switches may have push-in fittings in addition to the screw terminals. Some specialty switches (pages 50 to 51) have wire leads instead of screw terminals. They are connected to circuit wires with wire nuts.

A wall switch is connected to circuit wires with screw terminals or with push-in fittings on the back of the switch. A switch may have a stamped strip gauge that indicates how much insulation must be stripped from the circuit wires to make the connections.

The switch body is attached to a metal mounting strap that allows it to be mounted in an electrical box. Several rating stamps are found on the strap and on the back of the switch. The abbreviation UL or UND. LAB. INC. LIST means that the switch meets the safety standards of the Underwriters Laboratories. Switches also are stamped with maximum voltage and amperage ratings. Standard wall switches are rated 15A, 125V. Voltage ratings of 110, 120, and 125 are considered to be identical for purposes of identification.

For standard wall switch installations, choose a switch that has a wire gauge rating of #12 or #14. For wire systems with solid-core copper wiring, use only switches marked COPPER or CU. For aluminum wiring (page 22), use only switches marked CO/ALR. Switches marked AL/CU can no longer be used with aluminum wiring, according to the National Electrical Code.

Single-pole Wall Switches

A single-pole switch is the most common type of wall switch. It usually has ON-OFF markings on the switch lever, and is used to control a set of lights, an appliance, or a receptacle from a single location. A single-pole switch has two screw terminals. Some types also may have a grounding screw. When installing a single-pole switch, check to make sure the ON marking shows when the switch lever is in the up position.

In a correctly wired single-pole switch, a hot circuit wire is attached to each screw terminal. However, the color and number of wires inside the switch box will vary, depending on the location of the switch along the electrical circuit.

If two cables enter the box, then the switch lies in the middle of the circuit. In this installation, both of the hot wires attached to the switch are black.

If only one cable enters the box, then the switch lies at the end of the circuit. In this installation (sometimes called a switch loop), one of the hot wires is black, but the other hot wire usually is white. A white hot wire sometimes is coded with black tape or paint.

NOTE: Position of the screw terminals on switch may vary, depending on manufacturer

Switch lever

Two screw terminals

Typical Single-pole Switch Installations

Grounding wires   Cables

Grounding wire   Cable

Two cables enter the box when a switch is located in the middle of a circuit. Each cable has a white and a black insulated wire, plus a bare copper grounding wire. The black wires are hot, and are connected to the screw terminals on the switch. The white wires are neutral and are joined together with a wire nut. Grounding wires are pigtailed to the grounded box.

One cable enters the box when a switch is located at the end of a circuit. The cable has a white and a black insulated wire, plus a bare copper grounding wire. In this installation, both of the insulated wires are hot. The white wire may be labeled with black tape or paint to identify it as a hot wire. The grounding wire is connected to the grounded metal box.

NOTE: Position of the screw terminals on switch may vary, depending on manufacturer

Common screw terminal

Traveler screw terminals

Three-way Wall Switches

Three-way switches have three screw terminals, and do not have ON-OFF markings. Three-way switches are always installed in pairs, and are used to control a set of lights from two locations.

One of the screw terminals on a three-way switch is darker than the others. This screw is the **common screw terminal.** The position of the common screw terminal on the switch body may vary, depending on the manufacturer. Before disconnecting a three-way switch, always label the wire that is connected to the common screw terminal. It must be reconnected to the common screw terminal on the new switch.

The two lighter-colored screw terminals on a three-way switch are called the **traveler screw terminals.** The traveler terminals are interchangeable, so there is no need to label the wires attached to them.

Because three-way switches are installed in pairs, it sometimes is difficult to determine which of the switches is causing a problem. The switch that receives greater use is more likely to fail, but you may need to inspect both switches to find the source of the problem.

Typical Three-way Switch Installations

Traveler screw terminals

Grounding wires

Two-wire cable

Common screw terminal

Three-wire cable

Traveler screw terminals

Common screw terminal

Grounding wire

Two cables enter box if the switch lies in the middle of a circuit. One cable has two wires, plus a bare copper grounding wire; the other cable has three wires, plus a ground. The black wire from the two-wire cable is connected to the dark, common screw terminal. The red and black wires from the three-wire cable are connected to the traveler screw terminals. The white neutral wires are joined together with a wire nut, and the grounding wires are pigtailed to the grounded metal box.

One cable enters the box if the switch lies at the end of the circuit. The cable has a black wire, red wire, and white wire, plus a bare copper grounding wire. The black wire must be connected to the common screw terminal, which is darker than the other two screw terminals. The white and red wires are connected to the two traveler screw terminals. The bare copper grounding wire is connected to the grounded metal box.

Four-way Wall Switches

Four-way switches have four screw terminals, and do not have ON-OFF markings. Four-way switches are always installed between a pair of three-way switches. This switch combination makes it possible to control a set of lights from three or more locations. Four-way switches are not common, but are sometimes found in homes that have very large rooms or long hallways. Switch problems in a four-way installation can be caused by loose connections or worn parts in a four-way switch or in one of the three-way switches (page opposite).

In a typical installation, two pairs of color-matched wires are connected to the four-way switch. To simplify installation, newer four-way switches have screw terminals that are paired by color. One pair of screws usually is copper, while the other pair is brass. When installing the switch, match the wires to the screw terminals by color. For example, if a red wire is connected to one of the brass screw terminals, make sure the other red wire is connected to the remaining brass screw terminal.

Brass screw terminals

NOTE: Position of the screw terminals on switch may vary, depending on manufacturer

Copper screw terminals

Typical Four-way Switch Installation

Brass screw terminals

Grounding wires

Copper screw terminals

Four wires are connected to a four-way switch. One pair of color-matched wires is connected to the copper screw terminals, while another pair is connected to the brass screw terminals. A third pair of wires are connected inside the box with a wire nut. The two bare copper grounding wires are pigtailed to the grounded metal box.

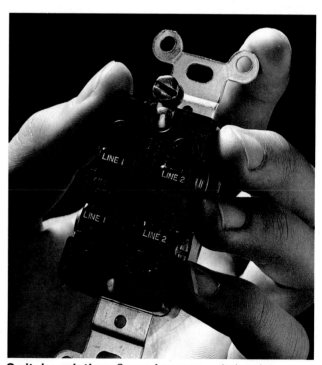

Switch variation: Some four-way switches have a wiring guide stamped on the back to help simplify installation. For the switch shown above, one pair of color-matched circuit wires will be connected to the screw terminals marked LINE 1, while the other pair of wires will be attached to the screw terminals marked LINE 2.

Single-circuit wiring: Three black wires are attached to the switch. The black feed wire bringing power into the box is connected to the side of the switch that has a connecting tab. The wires carrying power out to the light fixtures or appliances are connected to the side of the switch that **does not** have a connecting tab. The white neutral wires are connected together with a wire nut.

Double Switches

A double switch has two switch levers in a single housing. It is used to control two light fixtures or appliances from the same switch box.

In most installations, both halves of the switch are powered by the same circuit. In these **single-circuit** installations, three wires are connected to the double switch. One wire, called the "feed" wire, supplies power to both halves of the switch. The other wires carry power out to the individual light fixtures or appliances.

In rare installations, each half of the switch is powered by a separate circuit. In these **separate-circuit** installations, four wires are connected to the switch, and the metal connecting tab joining two of the screw terminals is removed (photo below).

Separate-circuit wiring: Four black wires are attached to the switch. Feed wires from the power source are attached to the side of switch that has a connecting tab, and the connecting tab is removed (photo, right). Wires carrying power from the switch to light fixtures or appliances are connected to the side of the switch that **does not** have a connecting tab. White neutral wires are connected together with a wire nut.

Remove the connecting tab on a double switch when wired in a separate-circuit installation. The tab can be removed with needle-nose pliers or a screwdriver.

Pilot-light Switches

A pilot-light switch has a built-in bulb that glows when power flows through the switch to a light fixture or appliance. Pilot-light switches often are installed for convenience if a light fixture or appliance cannot be seen from the switch location. Basement lights, garage lights, and attic exhaust fans frequently are controlled by pilot-light switches.

A pilot-light switch requires a neutral wire connection. A switch box that contains a single two-wire cable has only hot wires, and cannot be fitted with a pilot-light switch.

Pilot-light switch wiring: Three wires are connected to the switch. One black wire is the feed wire that brings power into the box. It is connected to the brass screw terminal on the side of the switch that **does not** have a connecting tab. The white neutral wires are pigtailed to the silver screw terminal. Black wire carrying power out to light fixture or appliance is connected to screw terminal on side of the switch that has a connecting tab.

Switch/receptacles

A switch/receptacle combines a grounded receptacle with a single-pole wall switch. In a room that does not have enough wall receptacles, electrical service can be improved by replacing a single-pole switch with a switch/receptacle.

A switch/receptacle requires a neutral wire connection. A switch box that contains a single two-wire cable has only hot wires, and cannot be fitted with a switch/receptacle.

A switch/receptacle can be installed in one of two ways. In the most common installations, the receptacle is hot even when the switch is off (photo, right).

In rare installations, a switch/-receptacle is wired so the receptacle is hot only when the switch is on. In this installation, the hot wires are reversed, so that the feed wire is attached to the brass screw terminal on the side of the switch that does not have a connecting tab.

Switch/receptacle wiring: Three wires are connected to the switch/-receptacle. One of the hot wires is the feed wire that brings power into the box. It is connected to the side of the switch that has a connecting tab. The other hot wire carries power out to the light fixture or appliance. It is connected to the brass screw terminal on the side that **does not** have a connecting tab. The white neutral wire is pigtailed to the silver screw terminal. The grounding wires must be pigtailed to the green grounding screw on the switch/receptacle and to the grounded metal box.

Specialty Switches

Specialty switches are available in several types. **Dimmer switches** (pages 60 to 61) are used frequently to control light intensity in dining and recreation areas. **Timer switches** and **time-delay switches** (below) are used to control light fixtures and exhaust fans automatically. New **electronic switches** (page opposite) provide added convenience and home security, and are easy to install. Electronic switches are durable, and they rarely need repair.

Most standard single-pole switches can be replaced with a specialty switch. Most specialty switches have preattached wire leads instead of screw terminals, and are connected to circuit wires with wire nuts. Some motor-driven timer switches require a neutral wire connection, and cannot be installed in switch boxes that have only one cable with two hot wires.

If a specialty switch is not operating correctly, you may be able to test it with a continuity tester (pages 52 to 55). Timer switches and time-delay switches can be tested for continuity, but dimmer switches cannot be tested. With electronic switches, the manual switch can be tested for continuity (page 55), but the automatic features cannot be tested.

Timer Switches

Timer switches have an electrically powered control dial that can be set to turn lights on and off automatically once each day. They are commonly used to control outdoor light fixtures.

Timer switches have three preattached wire leads. The black wire lead is connected to the hot feed wire that brings power into the box, and the red lead is connected to the wire carrying power out to the light fixture. The remaining wire lead is the neutral lead. It must be connected to any neutral circuit wires. A switch box that contains only one cable has no neutral wires, so it cannot be fitted with a timer switch.

After a power failure, the dial on a timer switch must be reset to the proper time.

Time-delay Switches

A time-delay switch has a spring-driven dial that is wound by hand. The dial can be set to turn off a light fixture after a delay ranging from 1 to 60 minutes. Time-delay switches often are used for exhaust fans, electric space heaters, bathroom vent fans, and heat lamps.

The black wire leads on the switch are connected to the hot circuit wires. If the switch box contains white neutral wires, these are connected together with a wire nut. The bare copper grounding wires are pigtailed to the grounded metal box.

A time-delay switch needs no neutral wire connection, so it can be fitted in a switch box that contains either one or two cables.

Automatic Switches

An automatic switch uses a narrow infrared beam to detect movement. When a hand passes within a few inches of the beam, an electronic signal turns the switch on or off. Some automatic switches have a manual dimming feature.

Automatic switches can be installed wherever a standard single-pole switch is used. Automatic switches are especially convenient for children and handicapped individuals.

Automatic switches require no neutral wire connections. For this reason, an automatic switch can be installed in a switch box containing either one or two cables. The wire leads on the switch are connected to hot circuit wires with wire nuts.

Motion-sensor Security Switches

A motion-sensor switch uses a wide-angle infrared beam to detect movement over a large area, and turns on a light fixture automatically. A time-delay feature turns off lights after movement stops.

Most motion-sensor switches have an override feature that allows the switch to be operated manually. Better switches include an adjustable sensitivity control, and a variable time-delay shutoff control.

Motion-sensor switches require no neutral wire connections. They can be installed in switch boxes containing either one or two cables. The wire leads on the switch are connected to hot circuit wires with wire nuts.

Programmable Switches

Programmable switches represent the latest in switch design. They have digital controls, and can provide four on-off cycles each day.

Programmable switches frequently are used to provide security when a homeowner is absent from the house. Law enforcement experts say that programmed lighting is a proven crime deterrent. For best protection, programmable switches should be set to a random on-off pattern.

Programmable switches require no neutral wire connections. They can be installed in switch boxes containing either one or two cables. The wire leads on the switch are connected to hot circuit wires with wire nuts.

Testing Switches for Continuity

A switch that does not work properly may have worn or broken internal parts. Test for internal wear with a battery-operated continuity tester. The continuity tester detects any break in the metal pathway inside the switch. Replace the switch if the continuity tester shows the switch to be faulty.

Never use a continuity tester on wires that might carry live current. Always shut off the power and disconnect the switch before testing for continuity.

Some specialty switches, like dimmers, cannot be tested for continuity. Electronic switches can be tested for manual operation using a continuity tester, but the automatic operation of these switches cannot be tested.

Everything You Need:

Tools: continuity tester.

How to Test a Single-pole Wall Switch

Attach clip of tester to one of the screw terminals. Touch the tester probe to the other screw terminal. Flip switch lever from ON to OFF. If switch is good, tester glows when lever is ON, but not when OFF.

Continuity tester uses battery-generated current to test the metal pathways running through switches and other electrical fixtures. Always "test" the tester before use. Touch the tester clip to the metal probe. The tester should glow. If not, then the battery or light bulb is dead and must be replaced.

How to Test a Three-way Wall Switch

Traveler screw terminals

Common screw terminal

1 Attach tester clip to the dark common screw terminal. Touch the tester probe to one of the traveler screw terminals, and flip switch lever back and forth. If switch is good, the tester should glow when the lever is in one position, but not both.

2 Touch probe to the other traveler screw terminal, and flip the switch lever back and forth. If switch is good, the tester will glow only when the switch lever is in the position opposite from the positive test in step 1.

How to Test a Four-way Wall Switch

A   B

C   D

1 Test switch by touching probe and clip of continuity tester to each pair of screw terminals (A-B, C-D, A-D, B-C, A-C, B-D). The test should show continuous pathways between two different pairs of screw terminals. Flip lever to opposite position, and repeat test. Test should show continuous pathways between two different pairs of screw terminals.

2 If switch is good, test will show a total of four continuous pathways between screw terminals — two pathways for each lever position. If not, then switch is faulty and must be replaced. (The arrangement of the pathways may differ, depending on the switch manufacturer. The photo above shows the three possible pathway arrangements.)

How to Test a Pilot-light Switch

1 Test pilot light by flipping the switch lever to the ON position. Check to see if the light fixture or appliance is working. If the pilot light does not glow even though the switch operates the light fixture or appliance, then the pilot light is defective and the unit must be replaced.

2 Test the switch by disconnecting the unit. With the switch lever in the ON position, attach the tester clip to the top screw terminal on one side of the switch. Touch tester probe to top screw terminal on opposite side of the switch. If switch is good, tester will glow when switch is ON, but not when OFF.

How to Test a Timer Switch

1 Attach the tester clip to the red wire lead on the timer switch, and touch the tester probe to the black hot lead. Rotate the timer dial clockwise until the ON tab passes the arrow marker. Tester should glow. If it does not, the switch is faulty and must be replaced.

2 Rotate the dial clockwise until the OFF tab passes the arrow marker. Tester should not glow. If it does, the switch is faulty and must be replaced.

How to Test Switch/receptacle

Attach tester clip to one of the top screw terminals. Touch the tester probe to the top screw terminal on the opposite side. Flip the switch lever from ON to OFF position. If the switch is working correctly, the tester will glow when the switch lever is ON, but not when OFF.

How to Test a Double Switch

Test each half of switch by attaching the tester clip to one screw terminal, and touching the probe to the opposite side. Flip switch lever from ON to OFF position. If switch is good, tester glows when the switch lever is ON, but not when OFF. Repeat test with the remaining pair of screw terminals. If either half tests faulty, replace the unit.

How to Test a Time-delay Switch

Attach tester clip to one of the wire leads, and touch the tester probe to the other lead. Set the timer for a few minutes. If switch is working correctly, the tester will glow until the time expires.

How to Test Manual Operation of Electronic Switches

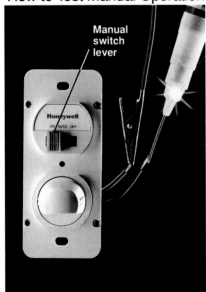

Automatic switch: Attach the tester clip to a black wire lead, and touch the tester probe to the other black lead. Flip the manual switch lever from ON to OFF position. If switch is working correctly, tester will glow when the switch lever is ON, but not when OFF.

Programmable switch: Attach the tester clip to a wire lead, and touch the tester probe to the other lead. Flip the manual switch lever from ON to OFF position. If the switch is working correctly, the tester will glow when the switch lever is ON, but not when OFF.

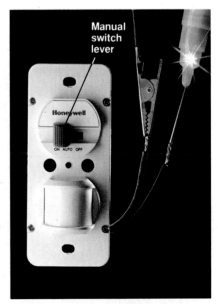

Motion-sensor switch: Attach the tester clip to a wire lead, and touch the tester probe to the other lead. Flip the manual switch lever from ON to OFF position. If the switch is working correctly, the tester will glow when the switch lever is ON, but not when OFF.

Fixing & Replacing Wall Switches

Most switch problems are caused by loose wire connections. If a fuse blows or a circuit breaker trips when a switch is turned on, a loose wire may be touching the metal box. Loose wires also can cause switches to overheat or buzz.

Switches sometimes fail because internal parts wear out. To check for wear, the switch must be removed entirely and tested for continuity (pages 52 to 55). If the continuity test shows the switch is faulty, replace it.

Everything You Need:

Tools: screwdriver, neon circuit tester, continuity tester, combination tool.

Materials: fine sandpaper, anti-oxidant paste (for aluminum wiring).

See Inspector's Notebook:
- Common Cable Problems (pages 112 to 113).
- Checking Wire Connections (pages 114 to 115).
- Electrical Box Inspection (pages 116 to 117).
- Inspecting Switches (page 121).

How to Fix or Replace a Single-pole Wall Switch

1 Turn off the power to the switch at the main service panel, then remove the switch coverplate.

2 Remove the mounting screws holding the switch to the electrical box. Holding the mounting straps carefully, pull the switch from the box. Be careful not to touch any bare wires or screw terminals until the switch has been tested for power.

3 Test for power by touching one probe of the neon circuit tester to the grounded metal box or to the bare copper grounding wire, and touching other probe to each screw terminal. Tester should not glow. If it does, there is still power entering the box. Return to service panel and turn off correct circuit.

4 Disconnect the circuit wires and remove the switch. Test the switch for continuity (page 52), and buy a replacement if the switch is faulty. If circuit wires are too short, lengthen them by adding pigtail wires (page 116).

5 If wires are broken or nicked, clip off damaged portion, using a combination tool. Strip wires so there is about ¾" of bare wire at the end of each wire.

6 Clean the bare copper wires with fine sandpaper if they appear darkened or dirty. If wires are aluminum, apply an anti-oxidant paste before connecting the wires.

7 Connect the wires to the screw terminals on the switch. Tighten the screws firmly, but do not overtighten. Overtightening may strip the screw threads

8 Remount the switch, carefully tucking the wires inside the box. Reattach the switch coverplate and turn on the power to the switch at the main service panel.

How to Fix or Replace a Three-way Wall Switch

1 Turn off power to the switch at the main service panel, then remove the switch coverplate and mounting screws. Holding the mounting strap carefully, pull the switch from the box. Be careful not to touch the bare wires or screw terminals until they have been tested for power.

2 Test for power by touching one probe of the neon circuit tester to the grounded metal box or to the bare copper grounding wire, and touching the other probe to each screw terminal. Tester should not glow. If it does, there is still power entering the box. Return to the service panel and turn off the correct circuit.

3 Locate dark common screw terminal, and use masking tape to label the "common" wire attached to it. Disconnect wires and remove switch. Test switch for continuity (page 53). If it tests faulty, buy a replacement. Inspect wires for nicks and scratches. If necessary, clip damaged wires and strip them (page 23).

4 Connect the common wire to the dark common screw terminal on the switch. On most three-way switches the common screw terminal is copper. Or, it may be labeled with the word COMMON stamped on the back of the switch.

5 Connect the remaining wires to the brass or silver screw terminals. These wires are interchangeable, and can be connected to either screw terminal. Carefully tuck the wires into the box. Remount the switch, and attach the coverplate. Turn on the power at the main service panel.

How to Fix or Replace a Four-way Wall Switch

1 Turn off the power to the switch at the main service panel, then remove the switch coverplate and mounting screws. Holding the mounting strap carefully, pull the switch from the box. Be careful not to touch any bare wires or screw terminals until they have been tested for power.

2 Test for power by touching one probe of the circuit tester to the grounded metal box or bare copper grounding wire, and touching the other probe to each of the screw terminals. Tester should not glow. If it does, there is still power entering the box. Return to the service panel and turn off the correct circuit.

3 Disconnect the wires and inspect them for nicks and scratches. If necessary, clip damaged wires and strip them (page 23). Test the switch for continuity (page 53). Buy a replacement if the switch tests faulty.

4 Connect two wires of the same color to the brass screw terminals. On the switch shown above, the brass screw terminals are labeled LINE 1.

5 Attach remaining wires to copper screw terminals, marked LINE 2 on some switches. Carefully tuck the wires inside the switch box, then remount the switch and attach the coverplate. Turn on the power at the main service panel.

Toggle-type dimmer resembles standard switches. Toggle dimmers are available in both single-pole and three-way designs.

Dial-type dimmer is the most common style. Rotating the dial changes the light intensity.

Slide-action dimmer has an illuminated face that makes the switch easy to locate in the dark.

Automatic dimmer has an electronic sensor that adjusts the light fixture to compensate for the changing levels of natural light. An automatic dimmer also can be operated manually.

Dimmer Switches

A dimmer switch makes it possible to vary the brightness of a light fixture. Dimmers are often installed in dining rooms, recreation areas, or bedrooms.

Any standard single-pole switch can be replaced with a dimmer, as long as the switch box is of adequate size. Dimmer switches have larger bodies than standard switches. They also generate a small amount of heat that must dissipate. For these reasons, dimmers should not be installed in undersized electrical boxes, or in boxes that are crowded with circuit wires. Always follow the manufacturer's specifications for installation.

In lighting configurations that use three-way switches (pages 46 to 47), one of the three-way switches can be replaced with a special three-way dimmer. In this arrangement, all switches will turn the light fixture on and off, but light intensity will be controlled only from the dimmer switch.

Dimmer switches are available in several styles (photo, left). All types have wire leads instead of screw terminals, and they are connected to circuit wires using wire nuts. A few types have a green grounding lead that should be connected to the grounded metal box or to the bare copper grounding wires.

Everything You Need:

Tools: screwdriver, neon circuit tester, needlenose pliers.

Materials: wire nuts, masking tape.

See Inspector's Notebook:
• Electrical Box Inspection (pages 116 to 117).

How to Install a Dimmer Switch

1 Turn off power to switch at the main service panel, then remove the coverplate and mounting screws. Holding the mounting straps carefully, pull switch from the box. Be careful not to touch bare wires or screw terminals until they have been tested for power.

2 Test for power by touching one probe of neon circuit tester to the grounded metal box or to the bare copper grounding wires, and touching other probe to each screw terminal. Tester should not glow. If it does, there is still power entering the box. Return to the service panel and turn off the correct circuit.

If replacing an old dimmer, test for power by touching one probe of circuit tester to the grounded metal box or bare copper grounding wires, and inserting the other probe into each wire nut. Tester should not glow. If it does, there is still power entering the box. Return to the service panel and turn off the correct circuit.

3 Disconnect the circuit wires and remove the switch. Straighten the circuit wires, and clip the ends, leaving about ½" of the bare wire end exposed.

4 Connect the wire leads on the dimmer switch to the circuit wires, using wire nuts. The switch leads are interchangeable, and can be attached to either of the two circuit wires.

Three-way dimmer has an additional wire lead. This "common" lead is connected to the common circuit wire. When replacing a standard three-way switch with a dimmer, the common circuit wire is attached to the darkest screw terminal on the old switch (page 58).

The earliest receptacles were modifications of the screw-in type light bulb. This receptacle was used in the early 1900s.

Common Receptacle Problems

Household receptacles, also called outlets, have no moving parts to wear out, and usually last for many years without servicing. Most problems associated with receptacles are actually caused by faulty lamps and appliances, or their plugs and cords. However, the constant plugging in and removal of appliance cords can wear out the metal contacts inside a receptacle. Any receptacle that does not hold plugs firmly should be replaced.

A loose wire connection is another possible problem. A loose connection can spark (called arcing), trip a circuit breaker, or cause heat to build up in the receptacle box, creating a potential fire hazard.

Wires can come loose for a number of reasons. Everyday vibrations caused by walking across floors, or from nearby street traffic, may cause a connection to shake loose. In addition, because wires heat and cool with normal use, the ends of the wires will expand and contract slightly. This movement also may cause the wires to come loose from the screw terminal connections.

The polarized receptacle became standard in the 1920s. The different sized slots direct current flow for safety.

The ground-fault circuit-interrupter, or GFCI receptacle, is a modern safety device. When it detects slight changes in current, it instantly shuts off power.

See Inspector's Notebook:

- Checking Wire Connections (pages 114 to 115).
- Electrical Box Inspection (pages 116 to 117).
- Inspecting Receptacles (page 120).

Problem	Repair
Circuit breaker trips repeatedly, or fuse burns out immediately after being replaced.	1. Repair or replace worn or damaged lamp or appliance cord. 2. Move lamps or appliances to other circuits to prevent overloads (page 34). 3. Tighten any loose wire connections (pages 72 to 73). 4. Clean dirty or oxidized wire ends (page 72).
Lamp or appliance does not work.	1. Make sure lamp or appliance is plugged in. 2. Replace burned-out bulbs. 3. Repair or replace worn or damaged lamp or appliance cord. 4. Tighten any loose wire connections (pages 72 to 73). 5. Clean dirty or oxidized wire ends (page 72). 6. Repair or replace any faulty receptacle (pages 72 to 73).
Receptacle does not hold plugs firmly.	1. Repair or replace worn or damaged plugs (pages 94 to 95). 2. Replace faulty receptacle (pages 72 to 73).
Receptacle is warm to the touch, buzzes, or sparks when plugs are inserted or removed.	1. Move lamps or appliances to other circuits to prevent overloads (page 34). 2. Tighten any loose wire connections (pages 72 to 73). 3. Clean dirty or oxidized wire ends (page 72). 4. Replace faulty receptacle (pages 72 to 73).

FRONT

Stamp of approval

Long (neutral) slot

Grounding hole

Voltage rating

Silver (neutral) screw terminals

Amperage rating

Green (grounding) screw terminal

Mounting strap

Short (hot) slot

Connecting tab

Push-in fitting

Wire ratings

Wire type

Brass (hot) screw terminals

BACK

The standard duplex receptacle has two halves for receiving plugs. Each half has a long (neutral) slot, a short (hot) slot, and a U-shaped grounding hole. The slots fit the wide prong, narrow prong, and grounding prong of a three-prong plug. This ensures that the connection between receptacle and plug will be polarized and grounded for safety (page 16).

Wires are attached to the receptacle at screw terminals or push-in fittings. A connecting tab between the screw terminals allows a variety of different wiring configurations. Receptacles also include mounting straps for attaching to electrical boxes.

Stamps of approval from testing agencies are found on the front and back of the receptacle. Look for the symbol UL or UND. LAB. INC. LIST to make sure the receptacle meets the strict standards of Underwriters Laboratories.

The receptacle is marked with ratings for maximum volts and amps. The common receptacle is marked 15A, 125V. Receptacles marked CU or COPPER are used with solid copper wire. Those marked CU-CLAD ONLY are used with copper-coated aluminum wire. Only receptacles marked CO/ALR may be used with solid aluminum wiring (page 22). Receptacles marked AL/CU no longer may be used with aluminum wire according to code.

Single cable entering the box indicates end-of-run wiring. The black hot wire is attached to a brass screw terminal, and the white neutral wire is connected to a silver screw terminal. If the box is metal, the grounding wire is pigtailed to the grounding screws of the receptacle and the box. In a plastic box, the grounding wire is attached directly to the grounding screw terminal of the receptacle.

Two cables entering the box indicate middle-of-run wiring. Black hot wires are connected to brass screw terminals, and white neutral wires to silver screw terminals. The grounding wire is pigtailed to the grounding screws of the receptacle and the box.

Receptacle Wiring

A 125-volt duplex receptacle can be wired to the electrical system in a number of ways. The most common are shown on these pages.

Wiring configurations may vary slightly from these photographs, depending on the kind of receptacle used, the type of cable, or the technique of the electrician who installed the wiring. To make dependable repairs or replacements, use masking tape and label each wire according to its location on the terminals of the existing receptacle.

Receptacles are wired as either **end-of-run** or **middle-of-run**. These two basic configurations are easily identified by counting the number of cables entering the receptacle box. End-of-run wiring has only one cable, indicating that the circuit ends. Middle-of-run wiring has two cables, indicating that the circuit continues on to other receptacles, switches, or fixtures.

A **split-circuit receptacle** is shown on the opposite page. Each half of a split-circuit receptacle is wired to a separate circuit. This allows two appliances of high wattage to be plugged into the same receptacle without blowing a fuse or tripping a breaker. This wiring configuration is similar to a receptacle that is controlled by a wall switch. Code requires a **switch-controlled receptacle** in any room that does not have a built-in light fixture operated by a wall switch.

Split-circuit and switch-controlled receptacles are connected to two hot wires, so use caution during repairs or replacements. Make sure the connecting tab between the hot screw terminals is removed.

Two-slot receptacles are common in older homes. There is no grounding wire attached to the receptacle, but the box may be grounded with armored cable or conduit (page 20).

White neutral wire

Grounding screw

Brass screw terminal

Black hot wire

Silver screw terminal

Connecting tab intact

Connecting tab removed

Red hot wire

Grounding wires

Grounding screw terminal

Single cable entering the box indicates end-of-run wiring

Split-circuit receptacle is attached to a black hot wire, a red hot wire, a white neutral wire, and a bare grounding wire. The wiring is similar to a switch-controlled receptacle.

The hot wires are attached to the brass screw terminals, and the connecting tab or fin between the brass terminals is removed. The white wire is attached to a silver screw terminal, and the connecting tab on the neutral side remains intact. The grounding wire is pigtailed to the grounding screw terminal of the receptacle, and to the grounding screw attached to the box.

Black hot wires

Silver screw terminal

Brass screw terminal

White neutral wires

Two cables entering the box indicate middle-of-run wiring

Two-slot receptacle is often found in older homes. The black hot wires are connected to the brass screw terminals, and the white neutral wires are pigtailed to a silver screw terminal.

Two-slot receptacles may be replaced with three-slot types, but only if a means of grounding exists at the receptacle box.

Basic Types of Receptacles

Several different types of receptacles are found in the typical home. Each has a unique arrangement of slots that accepts only a certain kind of plug, and each is designed for a specific job.

Household receptacles provide two types of voltage: normal and high voltage. Although voltage ratings have changed slightly over the years, normal receptacles should be rated for 110, 115, 120, or 125 volts. For purposes of replacement, these ratings are considered identical. High-voltage receptacles are rated at 220, 240, or 250 volts. These ratings are considered identical.

When replacing a receptacle, check the amperage rating of the circuit at the main service panel, and buy a receptacle with the correct amperage rating (page 28).

15 amps, 125 volts. Polarized two-slot receptacle is common in homes built before 1960. Slots are different sizes to accept polarized plugs.

15 amps, 125 volts. Three-slot grounded receptacle has two different size slots and a U-shaped hole for grounding. It is required in all new wiring installations.

20 amps, 125 volts. This three-slot grounded receptacle features a special T-shaped slot. It is installed for use with large appliances or portable tools that require 20 amps of current.

15 amps, 250 volts. This receptacle is used primarily for window air conditioners. It is available as a single unit, or as half of a duplex receptacle, with the other half wired for 125 volts.

30 amps, 125/250 volts. This receptacle is used for clothes dryers. It provides high-voltage current for heating coils, and 125-volt current to run lights and timers.

50 amps, 125/250 volts. This receptacle is used for ranges. The high-voltage current powers heating coils, and the 125-volt current runs clocks and lights.

Older Receptacles

Older receptacles may look different from more modern types, but most will stay in good working order. Follow these simple guidelines for evaluating or replacing older receptacles:

• Never replace an older receptacle with one of a different voltage or higher amperage rating.
• Any two-slot, unpolarized receptacle should be replaced with a two- or three-slot polarized receptacle.
• If no means of grounding is available at the receptacle box, install a GFCI (pages 74 to 77).
• If in doubt, seek the advice of a qualified electrician.

Never alter the prongs of a plug to fit an older receptacle. Altering the prongs may remove the grounding or polarizing features of the plug.

Unpolarized receptacles have slots that are the same length. Modern plug types may not fit these receptacles. Never modify the prongs of a polarized plug to fit the slots of an unpolarized receptacle.

Surface-mounted receptacles were popular in the 1940s and 1950s for their ease of installation. Wiring often ran in the back of hollowed-out base moldings. Surface-mounted receptacles are usually ungrounded.

Ceramic duplex receptacles were manufactured in the 1930s. They are polarized but ungrounded, and they can be wired for either 125 volts or 250 volts.

Twist-lock receptacles are designed to be used with plugs that are inserted and rotated. A small tab on the end of one of the prongs prevents the plug from being pulled from the receptacle.

Ceramic duplex receptacle has a unique hourglass shape. The receptacle shown above is rated for 250 volts but only 5 amps, and would not be allowed by today's electrical codes.

![Grounding wire, Red hot wire, Black hot wire, White neutral wire, Setscrew terminals labels]

A receptacle rated for 125/250 volts has two incoming hot wires, each carrying 125 volts, and a white neutral wire. A grounding wire is attached to the metal receptacle box. Connections are made with setscrew terminals at the back of the receptacle.

High-voltage Receptacles

High-voltage receptacles provide current to large appliances like clothes dryers, ranges, water heaters, and air conditioners. The slot configuration of a high-voltage receptacle (page 66) will not accept a plug rated for 125 volts.

A high-voltage receptacle can be wired in one of two ways. In a standard high-voltage receptacle, voltage is brought to the receptacle with two hot wires, each carrying a maximum of 125 volts. No white neutral wire is necessary, but a grounding wire should be attached to the receptacle and to the metal receptacle box.

A clothes dryer or range also may require normal current (a maximum of 125 volts) to run lights, timers and clocks. If so, a white neutral wire will be attached to the receptacle. The appliance itself will split the incoming current into a 125-volt circuit and a 250-volt circuit.

Repair or replace a high-voltage receptacle using the techniques shown on pages 72 to 73. It is important to identify and tag all wires on the existing receptacle so that the new receptacle will be properly wired.

Standard receptacle rated for 250 volts has two incoming hot wires and no neutral wire. A grounding wire is pigtailed to the receptacle and to the metal receptacle box.

Surface-mounted receptacle rated for 250 volts has a hard plastic box that can be installed on concrete or block walls. Surface-mounted receptacles are often found in basements and utility rooms.

Childproof Receptacles & Other Accessories

Childproof your receptacles or adapt them for special uses by adding receptacle accessories. Before installing an accessory, be sure to read the manufacturer's instructions.

Homeowners with small children should add inexpensive caps or covers to guard against accidental electric shocks.

Plastic caps do not conduct electricity and are virtually impossible for small children to remove. A receptacle cover attaches directly to the receptacle and fits over plugs, preventing the cords from being removed.

Protect children against the possibility of electrical shock. Place protective caps in any receptacles that are not being used.

Prevent accidents by installing a receptacle cover to prevent cords and plugs from being removed.

Install more than two plugs in a single duplex receptacle by using a multi-outlet power strip. A multi-outlet strip should have a built-in circuit breaker or fuse to protect against overloads.

Protect electronic equipment, such as a home computer or stereo, with a surge protector. The surge protector prevents any damage to sensitive wiring or circuitry caused by sudden drops or surges in power.

Recessed wall receptacle permits a plug-in clock to be hung flush against a wall surface.

Metal probes

Insulated handles

Bulb

Testing Receptacles for Power, Grounding & Polarity

Test for power to make sure that live voltage is not reaching the receptacle during a repair or replacement project.

Test for grounding to plan receptacle replacements. The test for grounding will indicate how an existing receptacle is wired, and whether a replacement receptacle should be a two-slot polarized receptacle, a grounded three-slot receptacle, or a GFCI.

If the test indicates that the hot and neutral wires are reversed (page 121), make sure the wires are installed correctly on the replacement receptacle.

Test for hot wires if you need to confirm which wire is carrying live voltage.

An inexpensive neon circuit tester makes it easy to perform these tests. It has a small bulb that glows when electrical power flows through it.

Remember that the tester only glows when it is part of a complete circuit. For example, if you touch one probe to a hot wire and do not touch anything with the other probe, the tester will not glow, even though the hot wire is carrying power. When using the tester, take care not to touch the metal probes.

When testing for power or grounding, always confirm any negative (tester does not glow) results by removing the coverplate and examining the receptacle to make sure all wires are intact and properly connected. Do not touch any wires without first turning off the power at the main service panel.

Everything You Need:

Tools: neon circuit tester, screwdriver.

How to Test a Receptacle for Power

1 Turn off power at the main service panel. Place one probe of the tester in each slot of the receptacle. The tester should not glow. If it does glow, the correct circuit has not been turned off at the main service panel. Test both ends of a duplex receptacle. Remember that this is a preliminary test. You must confirm that power is off by removing the coverplate and testing for power at the receptacle wires (step 2).

2 Remove the receptacle coverplate. Loosen the mounting screws and carefully pull the receptacle from its box. Take care not to touch any wires. Touch one probe of the neon tester to a brass screw terminal, and one probe to a silver screw terminal. The tester should not glow. If it does, you must shut off the correct circuit at the service panel. If wires are connected to both sets of terminals, test both sets.

Test a three-slot receptacle for grounding. With the power on, place one probe of the tester in the short (hot) slot, and the other in the U-shaped grounding hole. The tester should glow. If it does not glow, place a probe in the long (neutral) slot and one in the grounding hole. If the tester glows, the hot and neutral wires are reversed (page 121). If tester does not glow in either position, the receptacle is not grounded.

Test for hot wires. Occasionally, you may need to determine which wire is hot. With the power turned off, carefully separate all ends of wires so that they do not touch each other or anything else. Restore power to the circuit at the main service panel. Touch one probe of the neon tester to the bare grounding wire or grounded metal box, and the other probe to the ends of each of the wires. Check all wires. If the tester glows, the wire is hot. Label the hot wire for identification, and turn off power at the service panel before continuing work.

How to Test a Two-slot Receptacle for Grounding

1 With the power turned on, place one probe of the neon tester in each slot. The tester should glow. If it does not glow, then there is no power to the receptacle.

2 Place one probe of the tester in the short (hot) slot, and touch the other probe to the coverplate screw. The screw head must be free of paint, dirt, and grease. If the tester glows, the receptacle box is grounded. If it does not glow, proceed to step 3.

3 Place one probe of the tester in the long (neutral) slot, and touch the other to the coverplate screw. If the tester glows, the receptacle box is grounded but hot and neutral wires are reversed (page 121). If tester does not glow, the box is not grounded.

Repairing & Replacing Receptacles

Receptacles are easy to repair. After shutting off power to the receptacle circuit, remove the coverplate and inspect the receptacle for any obvious problems such as a loose or broken connection, or wire ends that are dirty or oxidized. Remember that a problem at one receptacle may affect other receptacles in the same circuit. If the cause of a faulty receptacle is not readily apparent, test other receptacles in the circuit for power (page 70).

When replacing a receptacle, check the amperage rating of the circuit at the main service panel, and buy a replacement receptacle with the correct amperage rating (page 34).

When installing a new receptacle, always test for grounding (pages 70 to 71). Never install a three-slot receptacle where no grounding exists. Instead, install a two-slot polarized, or GFCI receptacle.

Everything You Need:

Tools: neon circuit tester, screwdriver, vacuum cleaner (if needed).

Materials: fine sandpaper, anti-oxidant paste (if needed).

See Inspector's Notebook:
- Electrical Box Inspection (pages 116 to 117).
- Inspecting Switches & Receptacles (page 120).

How to Repair a Receptacle

1 Turn off power at the main service panel. Test the receptacle for power with a neon circuit tester (page 70). Test both ends of a duplex receptacle. Remove the coverplate, using a screwdriver.

2 Remove the mounting screws that hold the receptacle to the box. Carefully pull the receptacle from the box. Take care not to touch any bare wires.

3 Confirm that the power to the receptacle is off (page 70), using a neon circuit tester. If wires are attached to both sets of screw terminals, test both sets. The tester should not glow. If it does, you must turn off the correct circuit at the service panel.

4 If the ends of the wires appear darkened or dirty, disconnect them one at a time, and clean them with fine sandpaper. If the wires are aluminum, apply an anti-oxidant paste before reconnecting. Anti-oxidant paste is available at hardware stores.

5 Tighten all connections, using a screwdriver. Take care not to overtighten and strip the screws.

6 Check the box for dirt or dust and, if necessary, clean it with a vacuum cleaner and narrow nozzle attachment.

7 Reinstall the receptacle, and turn on power at the main service panel. Test the receptacle for power with a neon circuit tester. If the receptacle does not work, check other receptacles in the circuit before making a replacement.

How to Replace a Receptacle

1 To replace a receptacle, repeat steps 1 to 3 on the opposite page. With the power off, label each wire for its location on the receptacle screw terminals, using masking tape and a felt-tipped pen.

2 Disconnect all wires and remove the receptacle.

3 Replace the receptacle with one rated for the correct amperage and voltage (page 28). Replace coverplate, and turn on power. Test receptacle with a neon circuit tester (pages 70 to 71).

GFCI Receptacles

The ground-fault circuit-interrupter (GFCI) receptacle is a safety device. It protects against electrical shock caused by a faulty appliance, or a worn cord or plug. The GFCI senses small changes in current flow and can shut off power in as little as $\frac{1}{40}$ of a second.

When you are updating wiring, installing new circuits, or replacing receptacles, GFCIs are now required in bathrooms, kitchens, garages, crawl spaces, unfinished basements, and outdoor receptacle locations. GFCIs are easily installed as safety replacements for any standard duplex receptacle. Consult your local codes for any requirements regarding the installation of GFCI receptacles.

The GFCI receptacle may be wired to protect only itself (single location), or it can be wired to protect all receptacles, switches, and light fixtures from the GFCI "forward" to the end of the circuit (multiple locations). The GFCI cannot protect those devices that exist between the GFCI location and the main service panel.

Because the GFCI is so sensitive, it is most effective when wired to protect a single location. The more receptacles any one GFCI protects, the more susceptible it is to "phantom tripping," shutting off power because of tiny, normal fluctuations in current flow.

Everything You Need:

Tools: neon circuit tester, screwdriver.

Materials: wire nuts, masking tape.

A GFCI wired for single-location protection
(shown from the back) has hot and neutral wires connected only to the screw terminals marked LINE. A GFCI connected for single-location protection may be wired as either an end-of-run or middle-of-run configuration (page 64).

A GFCI wired for multiple-location protection
(shown from the back) has one set of hot and neutral wires connected to the LINE pair of screw terminals, and the other set connected to the LOAD pair of screw terminals. A GFCI receptacle connected for multiple-location protection may be wired only as a middle-of-run configuration.

How to Install a GFCI for Single-location Protection

1 Shut off power to the receptacle at the main service panel. Test for power with a neon circuit tester (page 70). Be sure to check both halves of the receptacle.

2 Remove coverplate. Loosen mounting screws, and gently pull receptacle from the box. Do not touch wires. Confirm power is off with a circuit tester (page 70).

3 Disconnect all white neutral wires from the silver screw terminals of the old receptacle.

4 Pigtail all the white neutral wires together, and connect the pigtail to the terminal marked WHITE LINE on the GFCI (see photo on opposite page).

5 Disconnect all black hot wires from the brass screw terminals of the old receptacle. Pigtail these wires together and connect them to the terminal marked HOT LINE on the GFCI.

6 If a grounding wire is available, disconnect it from the old receptacle, and reconnect it to the green grounding screw terminal of the GFCI. Mount the GFCI in the receptacle box, and reattach the coverplate. Restore power and test the GFCI according to the manufacturer's instructions.

How to Install a GFCI for Multiple-location Protection

1 Use a map of your house circuits (pages 30 to 33) to determine a location for your GFCI. Indicate all receptacles that will be protected by the GFCI installation.

2 Turn off power to the correct circuit at the main service panel. Test all the receptacles in the circuit with a neon circuit tester to make sure the power is off. Always check both halves of each duplex receptacle.

3 Remove the coverplate from the receptacle that will be replaced with the GFCI. Loosen the mounting screws and gently pull the receptacle from its box. Take care not to touch any bare wires. Confirm the power is off with a neon circuit tester (page 70).

4 Disconnect all black hot wires. Carefully separate the hot wires and position them so that the bare ends do not touch anything. Restore power to the circuit at the main service panel. Determine which black wire is the "feed" wire by testing for hot wires (page 71). The feed wire brings power to the receptacle from the service panel. Use caution: This is a "live" wire test, and power will be turned on temporarily.

5 When you have found the hot feed wire, turn off power at the main service panel. Identify the feed wire by marking it with masking tape.

6 Disconnect the white neutral wires from the old receptacle. Identify the white feed wire and label it with masking tape. The white feed wire will be the one that shares the same cable as the black feed wire.

7 Disconnect the grounding wire from the grounding screw terminal of the old receptacle. Remove the old receptacle. Connect the grounding wire to the grounding screw terminal of the GFCI.

8 Connect the white feed wire to the terminal marked WHITE LINE on the GFCI. Connect the black feed wire to the terminal marked HOT LINE on the GFCI.

9 Connect the other white neutral wire to the terminal marked WHITE LOAD on the GFCI.

10 Connect the other black hot wire to the terminal marked HOT LOAD on the GFCI.

11 Carefully tuck all wires into the receptacle box. Mount the GFCI in the box and attach the coverplate. Turn on power to the circuit at the main service panel. Test the GFCI according to the manufacturer's instructions.

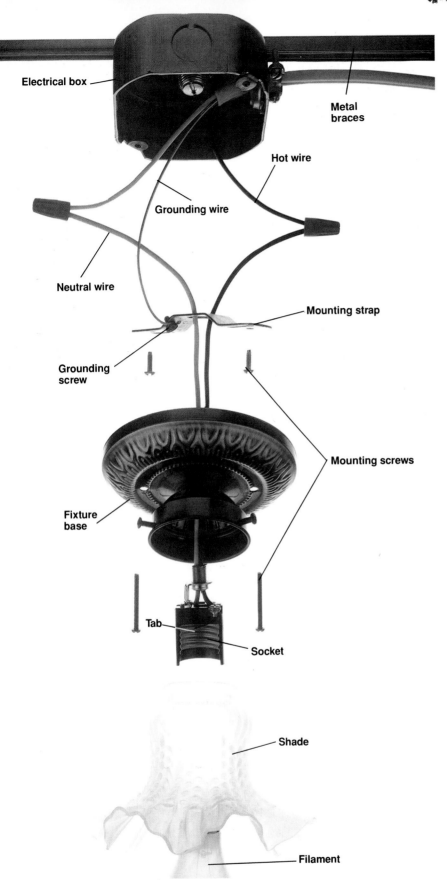

Repairing & Replacing Incandescent Light Fixtures

Electrical box

Metal braces

Hot wire

Grounding wire

Neutral wire

Mounting strap

Grounding screw

Mounting screws

Fixture base

Tab

Socket

Shade

Filament

In a typical incandescent light fixture, a black hot wire in the electrical box brings power to a small tab at the bottom of the metal socket. Power flows through a metal filament inside the bulb, causing it to heat up and glow. Power flows through the threaded portion of the socket and back to main service panel through the white neutral wire.

Incandescent light fixtures are attached permanently to ceilings or walls. They include wall-hung sconces, ceiling-hung globe fixtures, recessed light fixtures, and chandeliers. Most incandescent light fixtures are easy to repair, using basic tools and inexpensive parts.

Track lights, another type of incandescent light fixture, are difficult to fix and should be repaired or replaced by an electrician.

If a light fixture fails, always check the light bulb to make sure it is screwed in tightly and is not burned out. A faulty light bulb is the most common cause of light fixture failure. If the light fixture is controlled by a wall switch, also check the switch as a possible source of problems (pages 42 to 61).

Light fixtures can fail because the sockets or built-in switches wear out. Some fixtures have sockets that can be removed for minor repairs. These sockets are held to the base of the fixture with a mounting screw or clip. Other fixtures have sockets and switches that are joined permanently to the base. If this type of fixture fails, purchase and install a new light fixture.

Damage to light fixtures often occurs because homeowners install light bulbs with wattage ratings that are too high. Prevent overheating and light fixture failures by using only light bulbs that match the wattage ratings printed on the fixtures.

Techniques for repairing fluorescent lights are different from those for incandescent lights. Refer to pages 88 to 93 to repair or replace a fluorescent light fixture.

Everything You Need:

Tools: continuity tester, neon circuit tester, screwdrivers, combination tool.

Materials: replacement parts, as needed.

See Inspector's Notebook:
- Common Cable Problems (pages 112 to 113).
- Checking Wire Connections (pages 114 to 115).
- Electrical Box Inspection (pages 116 to 117).

Before 1959, incandescent lighting fixtures (shown cut away) often were mounted directly to an electrical box or to plaster lath. Electrical codes now require that lighting fixtures be attached to mounting straps that are anchored to the electrical boxes (page opposite). If you have a light fixture attached to plaster lath, install an approved electrical box with a mounting strap to support the fixture (pages 38 to 41).

Problem	Repair
Wall- or ceiling-mounted fixture flickers, or does not light.	1. Check for faulty light bulb. 2. Check wall switch, and repair or replace, if needed (pages 42 to 61). 3. Check for loose wire connections in electrical box . 4. Test socket, and replace, if needed (pages 80 to 81). 5. Replace light fixture (page 82).
Built-in switch on fixture does not work.	1. Check for faulty light bulb. 2. Check for loose wire connections on switch . 3. Replace switch (page 81). 4. Replace light fixture (page 82).
Chandelier flickers or does not light.	1. Check for faulty light bulb. 2. Check wall switch, and repair or replace, if needed (pages 42 to 61). 3. Check for loose wire connections in electrical box. 4. Test sockets, and replace, if needed (pages 86 to 87).
Recessed fixture flickers or does not light.	1. Check for faulty light bulb. 2. Check wall switch, and repair or replace, if needed (pages 42 to 61). 3. Check for loose wire connections in electrical box. 4. Test socket, and repair or replace, if needed (pages 83 to 84). 5. Replace recessed light fixture (page 85).

How to Remove a Light Fixture & Test a Socket

1 Turn off the power to the light fixture at the main service panel. Remove the light bulb and any shade or globe, then remove the mounting screws holding the fixture base to the electrical box or mounting strap. Carefully pull the fixture base away from box.

Grounding screw

2 Test for power by touching one probe of a neon circuit tester to green grounding screw, then inserting other probe into each wire nut. Tester should not glow. If it does, there is still power entering box. Return to the service panel and turn off power to correct circuit.

3 Disconnect the light fixture base by loosening the screw terminals. If fixture has wire leads instead of screw terminals, remove the light fixture base by unscrewing the wire nuts.

Metal tab

4 Adjust the metal tab at the bottom of the fixture socket by prying it up slightly with a small screwdriver. This adjustment will improve the contact between the socket and the light bulb.

Metal tab

Hot screw terminal

5 Test the socket (shown cut away) by attaching the clip of a continuity tester to the hot screw terminal (or black wire lead), and touching probe of tester to metal tab in bottom of socket. Tester should glow. If not, socket is faulty and must be replaced.

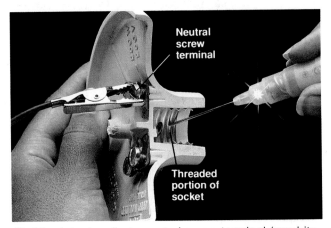

Neutral screw terminal

Threaded portion of socket

6 Attach tester clip to neutral screw terminal (or white wire lead), and touch probe to threaded portion of socket. Tester should glow. If not, socket is faulty and must be replaced. If socket is permanently attached, replace the fixture (page 82).

How to Replace a Socket

1 Remove light fixture (steps 1 to 3, page opposite). Remove the socket from the fixture. Socket may be held by a screw, clip, or retaining ring. Disconnect wires attached to the socket.

2 Purchase an identical replacement socket. Connect white wire to silver screw terminal on socket, and connect black wire to brass screw terminal. Attach socket to fixture base, and reinstall fixture.

How to Test & Replace a Built-in Light Switch

Retaining ring

Switch leads

1 Remove light fixture (steps 1 to 3, page opposite). Unscrew the retaining ring holding the switch.

2 Label the wires connected to the switch leads. Disconnect the switch leads and remove switch.

3 Test switch by attaching clip of continuity tester to one of the switch leads, and holding tester probe to the other lead. Operate switch control. If switch is good, tester will glow when switch is in one position, but not both.

4 If the switch is faulty, purchase and install an exact duplicate switch. Remount the light fixture, and turn on the power at the main service panel.

How to Replace an Incandescent Light Fixture

1 Turn off the power and remove the old light fixture, following the directions for standard light fixtures (page 80, steps 1 to 3) or chandeliers (pages 86 to 87, steps 1 to 4).

2 Attach a mounting strap to the electrical box, if box does not already have one. The mounting strap, included with the new light fixture, has a preinstalled grounding screw.

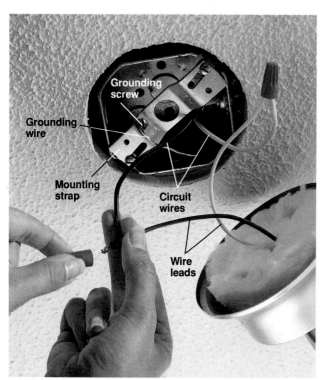

3 Connect the circuit wires to the base of new fixture, using wire nuts. Connect the white wire lead to the white circuit wire, and the black wire lead to the black circuit wire. Pigtail the bare copper grounding wire to the grounding screw on the mounting strap.

4 Attach the light fixture base to the mounting strap, using the mounting screws. Attach the globe, and install a light bulb with a wattage rating that is the same or lower than the rating indicated on the fixture. Turn on the power at the main service panel.

Repairing & Replacing Recessed Light Fixtures

Most problems with recessed light fixtures occur because heat builds up inside the metal canister and melts the insulation on the socket wires. On some recessed light fixtures, sockets with damaged wires can be removed and replaced. However, most newer fixtures have sockets that cannot be removed. With this type, you will need to buy a new fixture if the socket wires are damaged.

When buying a new recessed light fixture, choose a replacement that matches the old fixture. Install the new fixture in the metal mounting frame that is already in place.

Make sure building insulation is at least 3" away from the metal canister on a recessed light fixture. Insulation that fits too closely traps heat and can damage the socket wires.

How to Remove & Test a Recessed Light Fixture

1 Turn off the power to the light fixture at the main service panel. Remove the trim, light bulb, and reflector. The reflector is held to the canister with small springs or mounting clips.

2 Loosen the screws or clips holding the canister to the mounting frame. Carefully raise the canister and set it away from the frame opening.

3 Remove the coverplate on the wire connection box. The box is attached to the mounting frame between the ceiling joists.

(continued next page)

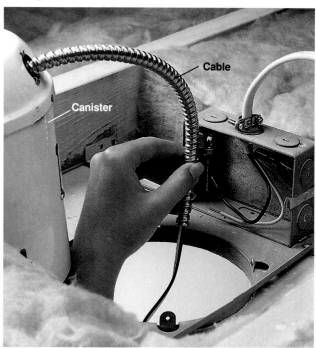

4 Test for power by touching one probe of neon circuit tester to grounded wire connection box, and inserting other probe into each wire nut. Tester should not glow. If it does, there is still power entering box. Return to the service panel and turn off correct circuit.

5 Disconnect the white and black circuit wires by removing the wire nuts. Pull the armored cable from the wire connection box. Remove the canister through the frame opening.

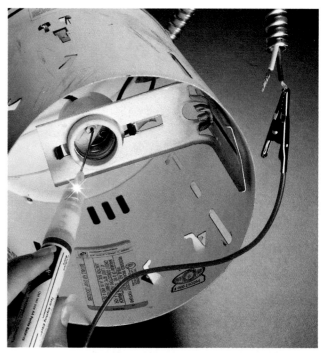

6 Adjust the metal tab at the bottom of the fixture socket by prying it up slightly with a small screwdriver. This adjustment will improve contact with the light bulb.

7 Test the socket by attaching the clip of a continuity tester to the black fixture wire and touching tester probe to the metal tab in bottom of the socket. Attach the tester clip to white fixture wire, and touch probe to the threaded metal socket. Tester should glow for both tests. If not, then socket is faulty. Replace the socket (page 81), or install a new light fixture (page opposite).

How to Replace a Recessed Light Fixture

1 Remove the old light fixture (pages 83 to 84). Buy a new fixture that matches the old fixture. Although new light fixture comes with its own mounting frame, it is easier to mount the new fixture using the frame that is already in place.

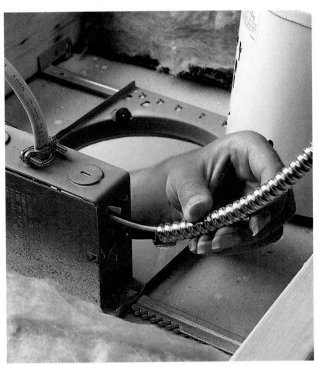

2 Set the fixture canister inside the ceiling cavity, and thread the fixture wires through the opening in the wire connection box. Push the armored cable into the wire connection box to secure it.

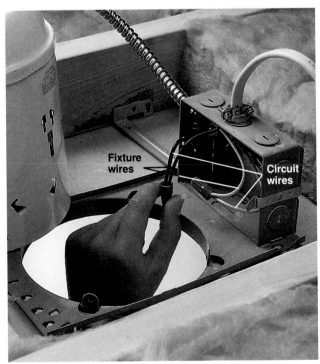

Fixture wires

Circuit wires

3 Connect the white fixture wire to the white circuit wire, and the black fixture wire to the black circuit wire, using wire nuts. Attach the coverplate to the wire connection box. Make sure any building insulation is at least 3" from canister and wire connection box.

4 Position the canister inside the mounting frame, and attach the mounting screws or clips. Attach the reflector and trim. Install a light bulb with a wattage rating that is the same or lower than rating indicated on the fixture. Turn on power at main service panel.

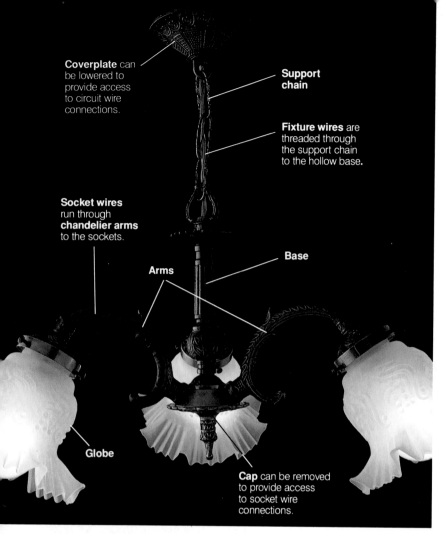

Coverplate can be lowered to provide access to circuit wire connections.

Support chain

Fixture wires are threaded through the support chain to the hollow base.

Socket wires run through **chandelier arms** to the sockets.

Arms

Base

Globe

Cap can be removed to provide access to socket wire connections.

Repairing Chandeliers

Repairing a chandelier requires special care. Because chandeliers are heavy, it is a good idea to work with a helper when removing a chandelier. Support the fixture to prevent its weight from pulling against the wires.

Chandeliers have two fixture wires that are threaded through the support chain from the electrical box to the hollow base of the chandelier. The socket wires connect to the fixture wires inside this base.

Fixture wires are identified as hot and neutral. Look closely for printed lettering or a colored stripe on one of the wires. This is the neutral wire that is connected to the white circuit wire and white socket wire. The other, unmarked, fixture wire is hot, and is connected to the black wires.

If you have a new chandelier, it may have a grounding wire that runs through the support chain to the electrical box. If this wire is present, make sure it is connected to the grounding wires in the electrical box.

How to Repair a Chandelier

1 Label any lights that are not working, using masking tape. Turn off power to the fixture at the main service panel. Remove light bulbs and all shades or globes.

Mounting strap

Threaded nipple

Coverplate

Retaining nut

2 Unscrew the retaining nut and lower the decorative coverplate away from the electrical box. Most chandeliers are supported by a threaded nipple attached to a mounting strap.

Mounting strap

Mounting bolt

Bolt cap nut

Mounting variation: Some chandeliers are supported only by the coverplate that is bolted to the electrical box mounting strap. These types do not have a threaded nipple.

3 Test for power by touching one probe of neon circuit tester to the green grounding screw, and inserting other probe into each wire nut. Tester should not glow. If it does, there is still power entering box. Return to service panel and turn off power to correct circuit.

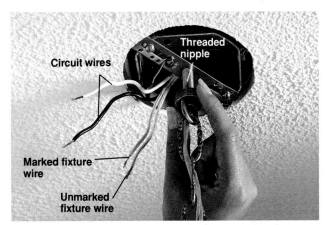

4 Disconnect fixture wires by removing the wire nuts. Marked fixture wire is neutral, and is connected to white circuit wire. Unmarked fixture wire is hot, and is connected to black circuit wire. Unscrew threaded nipple and carefully place chandelier on a flat surface.

5 Remove the cap from the bottom of the chandelier, exposing the wire connections inside the hollow base. Disconnect the black socket wires from the unmarked fixture wire, and disconnect the white socket wires from the marked fixture wire.

6 Test socket by attaching clip of continuity tester to black socket wire, and touching probe to tab in socket. Repeat test with threaded portion of socket and white socket wire. Tester should glow for both tests. If not, the socket is faulty and must be replaced.

7 Remove a faulty socket by loosening any mounting screws or clips, and pulling the socket and socket wires out of the fixture arm. Purchase and install a new chandelier socket, threading the socket wires through the fixture arm.

8 Test each fixture wire by attaching clip of continuity tester to one end of wire, and touching probe to other end. If tester does not glow, wire is faulty and must be replaced. Install new wires, if needed, then reassemble and rehang the chandelier.

Ballast

Socket

Fluorescent tube

Pins

Coverplate

Diffuser

A fluorescent light works by directing electrical current through a special gas-filled **tube** that glows when energized. A white transluscent **diffuser** protects the fluorescent tube and softens the light. A **coverplate** protects a special transformer, called a **ballast**. The ballast regulates the flow of 120-volt household current to the **sockets**. The sockets transfer power to metal **pins** that extend into the tube.

Repairing & Replacing Fluorescent Lights

Fluorescent lights are relatively trouble-free, and use less energy than incandescent lights. A typical fluorescent tube lasts about three years, and produces two to four times as much light per watt as a standard incandescent light bulb.

The most frequent problem with a fluorescent light fixture is a worn-out tube. If a fluorescent light fixture begins to flicker, or does not light fully, remove and examine the tube. If the tube has bent or broken pins, or black discoloration near the ends, replace it. Light gray discoloration is normal in working fluorescent tubes. When replacing an old tube, read the wattage rating printed on the glass surface, and buy a new tube with a matching rating.

Never dispose of old tubes by breaking them. Fluorescent tubes contain a small amount of hazardous mercury. Check with your local environmental control agency or health department for disposal guidelines.

Fluorescent light fixtures also can malfunction if the sockets are cracked or worn. Inexpensive replacement sockets are available at any hardware store, and can be installed in a few minutes.

If a fixture does not work even after the tube and sockets have been serviced, the ballast probably is defective. Faulty ballasts may leak a black, oily substance, and can cause a fluorescent light

Problem	Repair
Tube flickers, or lights partially.	1. Rotate tube to make sure it is seated properly in the sockets. 2. Replace tube (page 90) and the starter (where present) if tube is discolored or if pins are bent or broken. 3. Replace the ballast (page 92) if replacement cost is reasonable. Otherwise, replace the entire fixture (page 93).
Tube does not light.	1. Check wall switch, and repair or replace, if needed (pages 42 to 61). 2. Rotate the tube to make sure it is seated properly in sockets. 3. Replace tube (page 90) and the starter (where present) if tube is discolored or if pins are bent or broken. 4. Replace sockets if they are chipped, or if tube does not seat properly (page 91). 5. Replace the ballast (page 92) or the entire fixture (page 93).
Noticeable black substance around ballast.	Replace ballast (page 92) if replacement cost is reasonable. Otherwise, replace the entire fixture (page 93).
Fixture hums.	Replace ballast (page 92) if replacement cost is reasonable. Otherwise, replace the entire fixture (page 93).

fixture to make a loud humming sound. Although ballasts can be replaced, always check prices before buying a new ballast. It may be cheaper to purchase and install a new fluorescent fixture rather than to replace the ballast in an old fluorescent light fixture.

Everything You Need:

Tools: screwdriver, ratchet wrench, combination tool, neon circuit tester.

Materials: replacement tubes, starters, or ballast (if needed); replacement fluorescent light fixture (if needed).

See Inspector's Notebook:

• Common Cable Problems (pages 112 to 113).
• Checking Wire Connections (pages 114 to 115).
• Electrical Box Inspection (pages 116 to 117).

Older fluorescent lights may have a small cylindrical device, called a starter, located near one of the sockets. When a tube begins to flicker, replace both the tube and the starter. Turn off the power, then remove the starter by pushing it slightly and turning counterclockwise. Install a replacement that matches the old starter.

How to Replace a Fluorescent Tube

1 Turn off power to the light fixture at the main service panel. Remove the diffuser to expose the fluorescent tube.

2 Remove the fluorescent tube by rotating it ¼ turn in either direction and sliding the tube out of the sockets. Inspect the pins at the end of the tube. Tubes with bent or broken pins should be replaced.

3 Inspect the ends of the fluorescent tube for discoloration. New tube in good working order (top) shows no discoloration. Normal, working tube (middle) may have gray color. A worn-out tube (bottom) shows black discoloration.

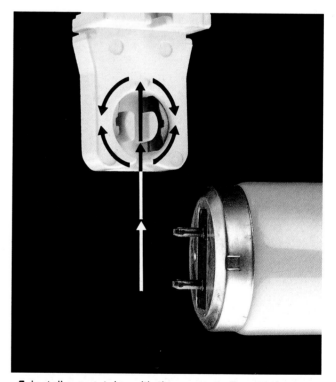

4 Install a new tube with the same wattage rating as the old tube. Insert the tube so that pins slide fully into sockets, then twist tube ¼ turn in either direction until it is locked securely. Reattach the diffuser, and turn on the power at the main service panel.

How to Replace a Socket

1 Turn off the power at the main service panel. Remove the diffuser, fluorescent tube, and the coverplate.

2 Test for power by touching one probe of a neon circuit tester to the grounding screw, and inserting the other probe into each wire nut. Tester should not glow. If it does, power is still entering the box. Return to the service panel and turn off correct circuit.

3 Remove the faulty socket from the fixture housing. Some sockets slide out, while others must be unscrewed.

4 Disconnect wires attached to socket. For push-in fittings (above) remove the wires by inserting a small screwdriver into the release openings. Some sockets have screw terminal connections, while others have preattached wires that must be cut before the socket can be removed.

5 Purchase and install a new socket. If socket has preattached wire leads, connect the leads to the ballast wires using wire nuts. Replace coverplate and diffuser, then turn on power at the main service panel.

How to Replace a Ballast

1 Turn off the power at the main service panel, then remove the diffuser, fluorescent tube, and coverplate. Test for power, using a neon circuit tester (step 2, page 91).

2 Remove the sockets from the fixture housing by sliding them out, or by removing the mounting screws and lifting the sockets out.

3 Disconnect the wires attached to the sockets by pushing a small screwdriver into the release openings (above), by loosening the screw terminals, or by cutting wires to within 2" of sockets.

4 Remove the old ballast, using a ratchet wrench or screwdriver. Make sure to support the ballast so it does not fall.

5 Install a new ballast that has the same ratings as the old ballast.

6 Attach the ballast wires to the socket wires, using wire nuts, screw terminal connections, or push-in fittings. Reinstall the coverplate, fluorescent tube, and diffuser. Turn on power to the light fixture at the main service panel.

How to Replace a Fluorescent Light Fixture

1 Turn off power to the light fixture at the main service panel. Remove diffuser, tube, and coverplate. Test for power, using a neon circuit tester (step 2, page 91).

2 Disconnect the insulated circuit wires and the bare copper grounding wire from the light fixture. Loosen the cable clamp holding the circuit wires.

3 Unbolt the fixture from the wall or ceiling, and carefully remove it. Make sure to support the fixture so it does not fall.

4 Position the new fixture, threading the circuit wires through the knockout opening in the back of the fixture. Bolt the fixture in place so it is firmly anchored to framing members.

5 Connect the circuit wires to the fixture wires, using wire nuts. Follow the wiring diagram included with the new fixture. Tighten the cable clamp holding the circuit wires.

6 Attach the fixture coverplate, then install the fluorescent tubes, and attach the diffuser. Turn on power to the fixture at the main service panel.

Faceplate

Grounded
round-cord
plug

Round-cord
plug

Flat-cord
plug

Quick-connect
plug

Polarized
plug

Underwriter's
knot

Replacing a Plug

Replace an electrical plug whenever you notice bent or loose prongs, a cracked or damaged casing, or a missing insulating faceplate. A damaged plug poses a shock and fire hazard.

Replacement plugs are available in different styles to match common appliance cords. Always choose a replacement that is similar to the original plug. Flat-cord and quick-connect plugs are used with light-duty appliances, like lamps and radios. Round-cord plugs are used with larger appliances, including those that have three-prong grounding plugs.

Some appliances use polarized plugs. A polarized plug has one wide prong and one narrow prong, corresponding to the hot and neutral slots found in a standard receptacle. Polarization (page 16) ensures that the cord wires are aligned correctly with the receptacle slots.

If there is room in the plug body, tie the individual wires in an underwriter's knot to secure the plug to the cord.

Everything You Need:

Tools: combination tool, needlenose pliers, screwdriver.

Materials: replacement plug.

How to Install a Quick-connect Plug

Casing

Core

1 Squeeze the prongs of the new quick-connect plug together slightly and pull the plug core from the casing. Cut the old plug from the flat-cord wire with a combination tool, leaving a clean-cut end.

2 Feed unstripped wire through rear of plug casing. Spread prongs, then insert wire into opening in rear of core. Squeeze prongs together; spikes inside core penetrate cord. Slide casing over core until it snaps into place.

Ridged half

Wide prong

When replacing a polarized plug, make sure that the ridged half of the cord lines up with the wider (neutral) prong of the plug.

How to Replace a Round-cord Plug

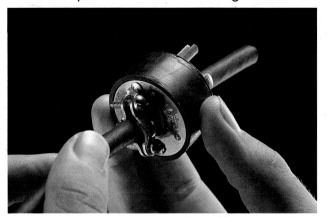

1 Cut off round cord near the old plug, using a combination tool. Remove the insulating faceplate on the new plug, and feed cord through rear of plug. Strip about 3" of outer insulation from the round cord. Strip ¾" insulation from the individual wires.

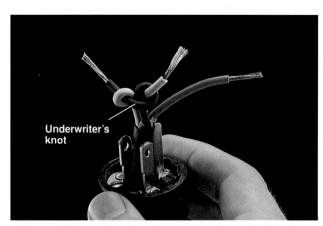

Underwriter's knot

2 Tie an underwriter's knot with the black and white wires. Make sure the knot is located close to the edge of the stripped outer insulation. Pull the cord so that the knot slides into the plug body.

3 Hook end of black wire clockwise around brass screw, and white wire around silver screw. On a three-prong plug, attach third wire to grounding screw. If necessary, excess grounding wire can be cut away.

4 Tighten the screws securely, making sure the copper wires do not touch each other. Replace the insulating faceplate.

How to Replace a Flat-cord Plug

Casing cover

1 Cut old plug from cord using a combination tool. Pull apart the two halves of the flat cord so that about 2" of wire are separated. Strip ¾" insulation from each half. Remove casing cover on new plug.

2 Hook ends of wires clockwise around the screw terminals, and tighten the screw terminals securely. Reassemble the plug casing. Some plugs may have an insulating faceplate that must be installed.

Circuit wires

Tuning bars

Magnetic coil

Plungers

Electrical box

Switch

Transformer

Low-voltage wires

Chimes

Home doorbell system is powered by a transformer that reduces 120-volt current to low-voltage current of 20 volts or less. Current flows from the transformer to one or more push-button switches. When pushed, the switch activates a magnetic coil inside the chime unit, causing a plunger to strike a musical tuning bar.

Fixing & Replacing Doorbells

Most doorbell problems are caused by loose wire connections or worn-out switches. Reconnecting loose wires or replacing a switch requires only a few minutes. Doorbell problems also can occur if the chime unit becomes dirty or worn, or if the low-voltage transformer burns out. Both parts are easy to replace. Because doorbells operate at low voltage, the switches and the chime unit can be serviced without turning off power to the system. However, when replacing a transformer, always turn off the power at the main service panel.

Most houses have other low-voltage transformers in addition to the doorbell transformer. These transformers control heating and air-conditioning thermostats (pages 102 to 109), or other low-voltage systems. When testing and repairing a doorbell system, it is important to identify the correct transformer. A doorbell transformer has a voltage rating of 20 volts or less. This rating is printed on the face of the transformer. A doorbell transformer often is located near the main service panel, and in some homes is attached directly to the service panel.

The transformer that controls a heating/air-conditioning thermostat system is located near the furnace, and has a voltage rating of 24 volts or more.

Occasionally, a doorbell problem is caused by a broken low-voltage wire somewhere in the system. You can test for wire breaks with a battery-operated multi-tester. If the test indicates a break, new low-voltage wires must be installed between the transformer and the switches, or between the switches and chime unit. Replacing low-voltage wires is not a difficult job, but it can be time-consuming. You may choose to have an electrician do this work.

Everything You Need:

Tools: continuity tester, screwdriver, multi-tester, needlenose pliers.

Materials: cotton swab, rubbing alcohol, replacement doorbell switch (if needed), masking tape, replacement chime unit (if needed).

How to Test a Doorbell System

1 Remove the mounting screws holding the doorbell switch to the house.

2 Carefully pull the switch away from the wall.

3 Check wire connections on the switch. If wires are loose, reconnect them to the screw terminals. Test the doorbell by pressing the button. If the doorbell still does not work, disconnect the switch and test it with a continuity tester.

4 Test the switch by attaching the clip of a continuity tester to one screw terminal, and touching the probe to the other screw terminal. Press the switch button. Tester should glow. If not, then the switch is faulty and must be replaced (page 100).

5 Twist the doorbell switch wires together temporarily to test the other parts of the doorbell system.

6 Locate the doorbell transformer, often located near the main service panel. Transformer may be attached to an electrical box, or may be attached directly to the side of the service panel.

Transformer

(continued next page)

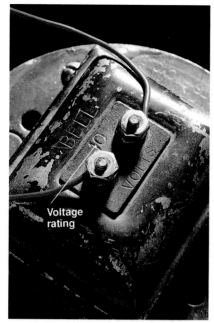

7 Identify the doorbell transformer by reading its voltage rating. Doorbell transformers have a voltage rating of 20 volts or less.

8 Turn off power to transformer at main service panel. Remove cover on electrical box, and test wires for power (step 3, page 107). Reconnect any loose wires. Replace taped connections with wire nut connections. Reattach coverplate.

9 Inspect the low-voltage wire connections, and reconnect any loose wires, using needlenose pliers. Turn on power to the transformer at the main service panel.

10 Set the dial of multi-tester to the 50-volt (AC) range.

11 Touch the probes of the multi-tester to the low-voltage screw terminals on the transformer.

12 If transformer is operating properly, multi-tester will detect power that is within 2 volts of transformer's rating. If not, then transformer is faulty and must be replaced (page 107).

13 Remove the coverplate on the doorbell chime unit.

 14 Inspect the low-voltage wire connections, and reconnect any loose wires.

 15 Test to make sure chime unit is receiving proper current with a multi-tester set to 50-volt (AC) range. Touch probes of tester to screw terminals marked TRANS-FORMER (or TRANS) and FRONT.

 16 If the multi-tester detects power within 2 volts of the transformer rating, then the chime unit is receiving proper current. If multi-tester detects no power, or very low power, then there is a break in the low-voltage wiring, and new wires must be installed.

 17 If necessary, repeat test for rear doorbell wires. Hold probes to terminals marked TRANS-FORMER (or TRANS) and REAR. Multi-tester should detect power within 2 volts of transformer's rating. If not, there is a break in wiring, and new wires must be installed.

 18 Clean the chime plungers with a cotton swab dipped in rubbing alcohol. Reassemble door-bell switches, then test the system by pushing one of the switches. If doorbell still does not work, then the chime unit is faulty and must be replaced (page 100).

How to Replace a Doorbell Switch

1 Remove the doorbell switch mounting screws, and carefully pull the switch away from the wall.

2 Disconnect wires from switch. Tape wires to the wall to prevent them from slipping into the wall cavity. Purchase a new doorbell switch, and connect wires to screw terminals on new switch. (Wires are interchangeable, and can be connected to either screw terminal.)

3 Anchor the switch to the wall with the mounting screws.

How to Replace a Doorbell Chime Unit

1 Turn off power to the doorbell system at the main service panel. Remove the coverplate from the old chime unit.

2 Using masking tape, label the low-voltage wires FRONT, REAR, or TRANS to identify their screw terminal locations. Disconnect the low-voltage wires.

3 Unscrew the mounting screws, and remove the old chime unit.

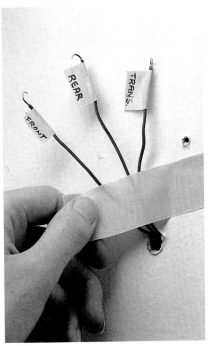

4 Tape the wires to the wall to prevent them from slipping into the wall cavity.

5 Purchase a new chime unit that matches the voltage rating of the old unit. Thread the low-voltage wires through the base of the new chime unit.

6 Attach the chime unit to the wall, using the mounting screws included with the installation kit.

7 Connect the low-voltage wires to the screw terminals on the new chime unit.

8 Attach the coverplate and turn on the power at the main service panel.

Electronic programmable thermostats can be set to make up to four temperature changes each day. They are available in low-voltage designs (right) for central heating/cooling systems, and in line-voltage designs (left) for electric baseboard heating. Most electronic programmable thermostats have an internal battery that saves the program in case of a power failure.

Fixing & Replacing Thermostats

A thermostat is a temperature-sensitive switch that automatically controls home heating and air-conditioning systems. There are two types of thermostats used to control heating and air-conditioning systems. **Low-voltage thermostats** control whole-house heating and air conditioning from one central location. **Line-voltage thermostats** are used in zone heating systems, where each room has its own heating unit and thermostat.

A low-voltage thermostat is powered by a transformer that reduces 120-volt current to about 24 volts. A low-voltage thermostat is very durable, but failures can occur if wire connections become loose or dirty, if thermostat parts become corroded, or if a transformer wears out. Some thermostat systems have two transformers. One transformer controls the heating unit, and the other controls the air-conditioning unit.

Line-voltage thermostats are powered by the same circuit as the heating unit, usually a 240-volt circuit. Always make sure to turn off the power before servicing a line-voltage thermostat.

A thermostat can be replaced in about one hour. Many homeowners choose to replace standard low-voltage or line-voltage thermostats with programmable setback thermostats. These programmable thermostats can cut energy use by up to 35%.

When buying a new thermostat, make sure the new unit is compatible with your heating/air-conditioning system. For reference, take along the brand name and model number of the old thermostat and of your heating/air-conditioning units. When buying a new low-voltage transformer, choose a replacement with voltage and amperage ratings that match the old thermostat.

Everything You Need:

Tools: soft-bristled paint brush, multi-tester, screwdriver, combination tool, neon circuit tester, continuity tester.

Materials: masking tape, short piece of wire.

Low-voltage thermostat system has a transformer that is either connected to an electrical junction box or mounted inside a furnace access panel. Very thin wires (18 to 22 gauge) send current to the thermostat. The thermostat constantly monitors room temperatures, and sends electrical signals to the heating/cooling unit through additional wires. The number of wires connected to the thermostat varies from two to six, depend-

ing on the type of heating/air-conditioning system. In the common four-wire system shown above, power is supplied to the thermostat through a single wire attached to screw terminal R. Wires attached to other screw terminals relay signals to the furnace heating unit, the air-conditioning unit, and the blower unit. Before removing a thermostat, make sure to label each wire to identify its screw terminal location.

Line-voltage thermostat for 240-volt baseboard heating unit usually has four wire leads, although some models have only two leads. On a four-wire thermostat, the two red wire leads (sometimes marked LINE

or L) are attached to the two hot feed wires bringing power into the box from the service panel. The black wire leads (sometimes marked LOAD) are connected to the circuit wires that carry power to the heating unit.

How to Inspect & Test a Low-voltage Thermostat System

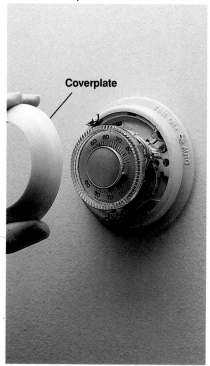

1 Turn off power to the heating/ air-conditioning system at the main service panel. Remove the thermostat coverplate.

2 Clean dust from the thermostat parts using a small, soft-bristled paint brush.

3 Remove the thermostat body by loosening the mounting screws with a screwdriver.

4 Inspect the wire connections on the thermostat base. Reattach any loose wires. If wires are broken or corroded, they should be clipped, stripped, and re-attached to the screw terminals (page 24).

5 Locate the low-voltage transformer that powers the thermostat. This transformer usually is located near the heating/air-conditioning system, or inside a furnace access panel. Tighten any loose wire connections.

6 Set the control dial of multi-tester meter to the 50-volt (AC) range. Turn on power to the heating/air-conditioning system at the main service panel.

7 Touch one probe of multi-tester to each of the low-voltage screw terminals. If tester does not detect current, then the transformer is defective and must be replaced (page 107).

8 Turn on power to heating system. Set thermostat control levers to AUTO and HEAT.

9 Strip ½" from each end of a short piece of insulated wire. Touch one end of the wire to terminal marked W and other end to terminal marked R. If heating system begins to run, then the thermostat is faulty, and must be replaced (page 106).

How to Install a Programmable Low-voltage Thermostat

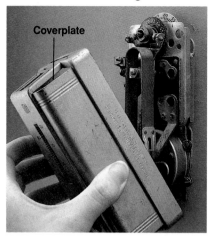

1 Turn off the power to the heating/air-conditioning system at the main service panel. Remove the thermostat coverplate.

2 Unscrew the thermostat mounting screws and remove the thermostat body.

3 Label the low-voltage wires to identify their screw terminal locations, using masking tape. Disconnect all low-voltage wires.

4 Remove the thermostat base by loosening the mounting screws. Tape the wires against the wall to make sure they do not fall into the wall cavity.

5 Thread the low-voltage wires through base of new thermostat. Mount the thermostat base on the wall, using the screws included with the thermostat.

6 Connect the low-voltage wires to the screw terminals on the thermostat base. Use the manufacturer's connection chart as a guide.

7 Install batteries in thermostat body, then attach the body to thermostat base. Turn on power and program the thermostat as desired.

How to Replace a Low-voltage Transformer

1 Turn off the power to the heating/air-conditioning system at the main service panel. Remove the coverplate on the transformer electrical box.

2 Carefully remove the wire nut connecting the black circuit wire to the transformer lead. Be careful not to touch bare wires.

3 Test for power by touching one probe of neon circuit tester to grounded metal box and other probe to exposed wires. Remove wire nut from white wires and repeat test. Tester should not glow for either test. If it does, power is still entering box. Return to service panel and turn off correct circuit.

4 Disconnect the grounding wires inside the box, then disconnect low-voltage wires attached to the screw terminals on the transformer. Unscrew the transformer mounting bracket inside the box, and remove transformer. Purchase a new transformer with the same voltage rating as the old transformer.

5 Attach new transformer to electrical box. Reconnect circuit wires to transformer leads. Connect circuit grounding wires to transformer grounding lead.

6 Connect the low-voltage wires to the transformer, and reattach the electrical box coverplate. Turn on the power at the main service panel.

How to Test & Replace a Line-voltage Thermostat

1 Turn off the power to the heating unit at the main service panel. Remove the thermostat coverplate.

2 Loosen the thermostat mounting screws, and carefully pull the thermostat from the electrical box.

3 Unscrew one wire nut. Test for power by touching one probe of neon circuit tester to grounded metal box and touching other probe to exposed wires. Tester should not glow. Repeat test with other wire connections. Tester should not glow. If it does, then power is still entering box. Return to service panel and turn off correct circuit.

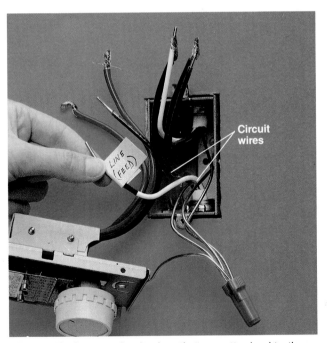

Circuit wires

4 Identify the two circuit wires that are attached to the thermostat leads marked LINE. These leads are often red. The circuit wires attached to the LINE leads bring power into the box, and are known as feed wires. Label the feed wires with masking tape, then disconnect all wires.

5 Test thermostat by attaching the clip of a continuity tester to one of the red wire leads, then touching probe to black wire lead on same side of thermostat. Turn temperature dial from HIGH to LOW. Tester should glow in both positions. Repeat test with other pair of wire leads. If tester does not glow for both positions, thermostat is faulty and must be replaced.

6 Replace a faulty thermostat with a new thermostat that has the same voltage and amperage ratings as the old one. Connect the new thermostat by attaching the circuit feed wires to the wire leads marked LINE, using wire nuts.

7 Connect the remaining circuit wires to the thermostat leads marked LOAD, using wire nuts. Connect the grounding wires together with a wire nut.

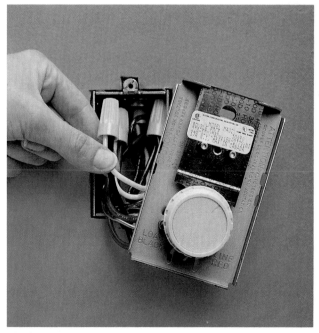

8 Carefully fold the wires inside the electrical box, then attach the thermostat mounting screws and the coverplate. Turn on the power at the main service panel. If new thermostat is programmable (page 102), set the program as desired.

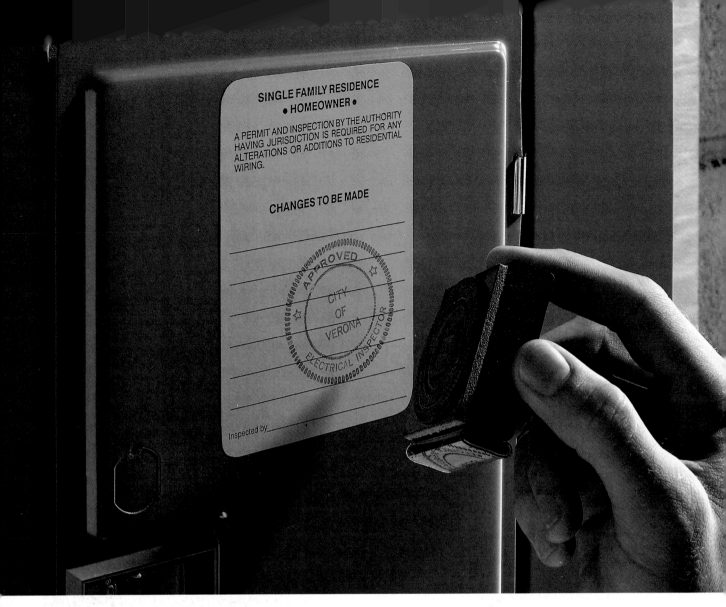

The following text appears within the image (inspection tag):

SINGLE FAMILY RESIDENCE
• HOMEOWNER •

A PERMIT AND INSPECTION BY THE AUTHORITY HAVING JURISDICTION IS REQUIRED FOR ANY ALTERATIONS OR ADDITIONS TO RESIDENTIAL WIRING.

CHANGES TO BE MADE

APPROVED
CITY OF VERONA
ELECTRICAL INSPECTOR

Inspected by

Inspector's Notebook

An electrical inspector visiting your home might identify a number of situations that are not "up to code." These situations may not be immediate problems. In fact, it is possible that the wiring in your home has remained trouble-free for many years.

Nevertheless, any wiring or device that is not up to code carries the potential for problems, often at risk to your home and your family. In addition, you may have trouble selling your home if it is not wired according to accepted methods.

Most local electrical codes are based on the National Electrical Code (NEC), a book updated and published every three years by the National Fire Protection Agency. This code book contains rules and regulations for the proper installation of electrical wiring and devices. Most public libraries carry reference copies of the NEC.

All electrical inspectors are required to be well versed in the NEC. Their job is to know the NEC regulations, and to make sure these rules are followed in order to prevent fires and ensure safety. If you have questions regarding your home wiring system, your local inspector will be happy to answer them.

While a book like Basic Wiring & Electrical Repairs cannot possibly identify all potential wiring problems in your house, we have created the "Inspector's Notebook" to help you identify some of the most common wiring defects and show you how to correct them. When working on home wiring repair or replacement projects, refer to this section to help identify any conditions that may be hazardous.

Service Panel Inspection

Problem: Rust stains are found inside the main service panel. This problem occurs because water seeps into the service head outside the house and drips down into the service panel.

Solution: Have an electrician examine the service head and the main service panel. If the panel or service wires have been damaged, new electrical service must be installed.

Inspecting the Grounding Jumper Wire

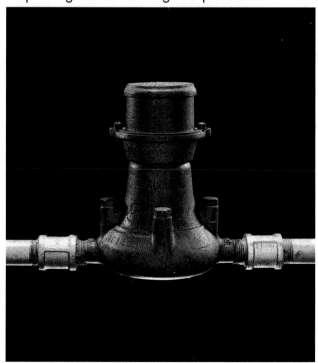

Problem: Grounding system jumper wire is missing or is disconnected. In most homes the grounding jumper wire attaches to water pipes on either side of the water meter. Because the ground pathway is broken, this is a dangerous situation that should be fixed immediately.

Solution: Attach a jumper wire to the water pipes on either side of the water meter, using pipe clamps. Use #6-gauge or #4-gauge bare copper wire for the jumper wire.

Common Cable Problems

Problem: Cable running across joists or studs is attached to the edge of framing members. Electrical codes forbid this type of installation in exposed areas, like unfinished basements or walk-up attics.

Solution: Protect cable by drilling holes in framing members at least 2" from exposed edges, and threading the cable through the holes.

Problem: Cable running along joists or studs hangs loosely. Loose cables can be pulled accidentally, causing damage to wires.

Solution: Anchor the cable to the side of the framing members at least 1¼" from the edge, using plastic staples. NM (nonmetallic) cable should be stapled every 4½ feet, and within 12" of each electrical box.

Problem: Cable threaded through studs or joists lies close to the edge of the framing members. NM (nonmetallic) cable (shown cut away) can be damaged easily if nails or screws are driven into the framing members during remodeling projects.

Cable shown cut away

Solution: Install metal nail guards to protect cable from damage. Nail guards are available at hardware stores and home centers.

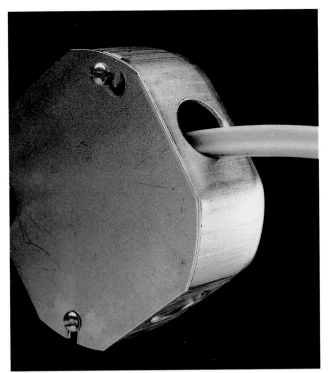

Problem: Unclamped cable enters a metal electrical box. Edges of the knockout can rub against the cable sheathing and damage the wires. (Note: with plastic boxes, clamps are not required if cables are anchored to framing members within 12" of box.)

Solution: Anchor the cable to the electrical box with a cable clamp (pages 38 to 39). Several types of cable clamps are available at hardware stores and home centers.

Problem: Cables are spliced outside an electrical box. Exposed splices can spark and create a risk of shock or fire.

Solution: Bring installation "up to code" by enclosing the splice inside a metal or plastic electrical box (pages 36 to 39). Make sure the box is large enough for the number of wires it contains.

Checking Wire Connections

Problem: Two or more wires are attached to a single screw terminal. This type of connection is seen in older wiring, but is now prohibited by the National Electrical Code.

Solution: Disconnect the wires from the screw terminal, then join them to a short length of wire (called a pigtail), using a wire nut (page 25). Connect the other end of the pigtail to the screw terminal.

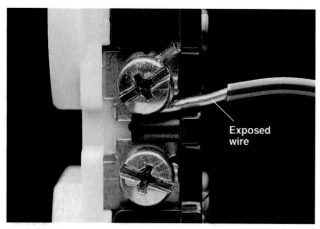

Exposed wire

Problem: Bare wire extends past a screw terminal. Exposed wire can cause a short circuit if it touches the metal box or another circuit wire.

Solution: Clip the wire and reconnect it to the screw terminal. In a proper connection, the bare wire wraps completely around the screw terminal, and the plastic insulation just touches the screw head (page 24).

Problem: Wires are connected with electrical tape. Electrical tape was used frequently in older installations, but it can deteriorate over time, leaving bare wires exposed inside the electrical box.

Solution: Replace electrical tape with wire nuts (page 25). You may need to clip away a small portion of the wire so the bare end will be covered completely by the wire nut.

114

Problem: No protective sleeve on armored cable. Sharp edges of the cable can damage the wire insulation, creating a shock hazard and fire risk.

Solution: Protect the wire insulation by installing plastic or fiber sleeves around the wires. Sleeves are available at hardware stores. Wires that are damaged must be replaced.

Problem: Nicks and scratches in bare wires interfere with the flow of current. This can cause the wires to overheat.

Solution: Clip away damaged portion of wire, then restrip about ¾" of insulation and reconnect the wire to the screw terminal (page 24).

Problem: Insulation on wires is cracked or damaged. If damaged insulation exposes bare wire, a short circuit can occur, posing a shock hazard and fire risk.

Solution: Wrap damaged insulation temporarily with plastic electrical tape. Damaged circuit wires should be replaced by an electrician.

Problem: Open electrical boxes create a fire hazard if a short circuit causes sparks (arcing) inside the box.

Solution: Cover the open box with a solid metal coverplate, available at any hardware store. Electrical boxes must remain accessible, and cannot be sealed inside ceilings or walls.

Problem: Short wires are difficult to handle. The National Electrical Code (NEC) requires that each wire in an electrical box have at least 6" of workable length.

Solution: Lengthen circuit wires by connecting them to short pigtail wires, using wire nuts (page 25). Pigtails can be cut from scrap wire, but should be the same gauge and color as the circuit wires.

Problem: Recessed electrical box is hazardous, especially if the wall or ceiling surface is made from a flammable material, like wood paneling. The National Electrical Code prohibits this type of installation.

Solution: Add an extension ring to bring the face of the electrical box flush with the surface. Extension rings come in several sizes, and are available at hardware stores.

Problem: Dust and dirt in electrical box can cause hazardous high-resistance short circuits (pages 122 to 125). When making routine electrical repairs, always check the electrical boxes for dust and dirt buildup.

Solution: Vacuum electrical box clean, using a narrow nozzle attachment. Make sure power to box is turned off at main service panel before vacuuming.

Problem: Crowded electrical box makes electrical repairs difficult. This type of installation is prohibited because wires can be damaged easily when a receptacle or switch is installed.

Solution: Replace the electrical box with a deeper electrical box (pages 36 to 39).

Problem: Light fixture is installed without an electrical box. This installation exposes the wiring connections, and provides no support for the light fixture.

Solution: Install an approved electrical box (pages 36 to 39) to enclose the wire connections and support the light fixture.

Common Electrical Cord Problems

Problem: Lamp or appliance cord runs underneath a rug. Foot traffic can wear off insulation, creating a short circuit that can cause fire or shock.

Solution: Reposition the lamp or appliance so the cord is visible. Replace worn cords.

Coverplate screw

Adapter

Metal loop

GFCI receptacle

Problem: Three-prong appliance plugs do not fit two slot receptacle. Do not use three-prong adapters unless the metal loop on the adapter is tightly connected to the coverplate screw on receptacle (page 17).

Solution: Install a three-prong grounded receptacle if a means of grounding exists at the box (pages 70 to 71). Install a GFCI (ground-fault circuit-interrupter) receptacle (pages 74 to 77) in kitchens and bathrooms, or if the electrical box is not grounded.

Problem: Lamp or appliance plug is cracked, or electrical cord is frayed near plug. Worn cords and plugs create a fire and shock hazard.

Solution: Cut away damaged portion of wire and install a new plug (pages 94 to 95). Replacement plugs are available at appliance stores and home centers.

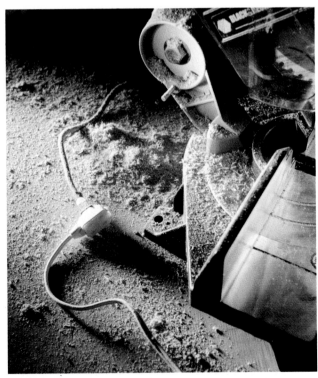

Problem: Extension cord is too small for the power load drawn by a tool or appliance. Undersized extension cords can overheat, melting the insulation and leaving bare wires exposed.

Solution: Use an extension cord with wattage and amperage ratings that meet or exceed the rating of the tool or appliance. Extension cords are for temporary use only. Never use an extension cord for a permanent installation.

Inspecting Receptacles & Switches

Problem: Octopus receptacle attachments used permanently can overload a circuit and cause overheating of the receptacle.

Solution: Use a multi-receptacle power strip with built-in overload protection. This is for temporary use only. If the need for extra receptacles is frequent, upgrade the wiring system.

Problem: Scorch marks near screw terminals indicate that electrical arcing has occurred. Arcing usually is caused by loose wire connections.

Solution: Clean wires with fine sandpaper, and replace the receptacle if it is badly damaged. Make sure wires are connected securely to screw teminals.

Problem: Two-slot receptacle in outdoor installation is hazardous because it has no grounding slot. In case of a short circuit, a person plugging in a cord becomes a conductor for current to follow to ground.

Solution: Install a GFCI (ground-fault circuit-interrupter) receptacle. Electrical codes now require that GFCIs be used for all outdoor receptacles, as well as for basement, kitchen, and bathroom receptacles.

Problem: White neutral wires are connected to switch. Although switch appears to work correctly in this installation, it is dangerous because light fixture carries voltage when the switch is off.

Solution: Connect the black hot wires to the switch, and join the white wires together with a wire nut.

Problem: White neutral wires are connected to the brass screw terminals on the receptacle, and black hot wires are attached to silver screw terminals. This installation is hazardous because live voltage flows into the long neutral slot on the receptacle.

Solution: Reverse the wire connections so that the black hot wires are attached to brass screw terminals and white neutral wires are attached to silver screw terminals. Live voltage now flows into the short slot on the receptacle.

Evaluating Old Wiring

If the wiring in your home is more than 30 years old, it may have a number of age-related problems. Many problems associated with older wiring can be found by inspecting electrical boxes for dirty wire connections (page 72), signs of arcing (page 120), cracked or damaged wire insulation (page 115), or dirt buildup (page 117).

However, it is difficult to identify problems with wiring that is hidden inside the walls. If old wires are dusty and have damaged insulation, they can "leak" electrical current. The amount of current that leaks through dust usually is very small, too small to trip a breaker or blow a fuse. Nevertheless, by allowing current to leave its normal path, these leaks consume power in much the same way that a dripping faucet wastes water.

This kind of electrical leak is called a high-resistance short circuit. A high-resistance short circuit can produce heat, and should be considered a fire hazard.

It is possible to check for high-resistance short circuits by using your electric meter to test the wires of each circuit. The goal of the test is to determine if electricity is being consumed even

if none of the lights and appliances are drawing power. To do this, you must turn on all wall switches to activate the hot circuit wires, then stop power consumption by removing light bulbs and fluorescent tubes, and disconnecting all lamps and appliances.

Then examine the electric meter, usually located on the outside of the house near the service head (page 12). If the flat, circular rotor inside the meter is turning, it means that a high-resistance short circuit is causing an electrical leak somewhere in the wiring. High-resistance short circuits consume very small amounts of power, so you should watch the rotor for a full minute to detect any movement.

If the test shows there is a high-resistance short circuit in your wiring, contact a licensed electrician to have it repaired.

Everything You Need:

Tools: screwdriver.

Materials: wire nuts, masking tape, pen.

How to Evaluate Old Wiring for High-resistance Short Circuits

1 Switch on all light fixtures. Remember to turn on closet lights, basement lights, and exterior lights.

2 Stop all power consumption by removing all light bulbs and fluorescent tubes. Turn off all thermostats.

3 Disconnect all plug-in lamps and appliances from the receptacles.

4 Shut off power to all permanently wired appliances by turning off the correct breakers or removing the correct fuses at the service panel. Permanently wired appliances include attic fans, water heaters, garage door openers, and ceiling fans.

5 With the power turned off, disconnect circuit wires from each permanently wired appliance. Cap the wire ends with wire nuts. Next, turn on power and make sure all appliance wall switches are turned on.

(continued next page)

How to Evaluate Old Wiring for High-resistance Short Circuits (continued)

6 Watch the circular rotor located inside the electric meter for at least one minute. If the rotor does not move, then your wiring is in good condition. If the rotor moves, it means there is a high-resistance short circuit somewhere in the wiring system: proceed to step 7.

7 Turn off power to all circuits at the main service panel by switching off circuit breakers or removing fuses. Do not turn off main shutoff. Watch the rotor inside the meter. If rotor moves, then the high-resistance short circuit is located in the main service panel or service wiring. In this case, consult a licensed electrician. If rotor does not move, proceed to step 8.

8 Turn on individual circuits, one at a time, by switching on the circuit breaker or inserting the fuse. Watch for rotor movement in the electric meter. If rotor does not move, wiring is in good condition. Turn off power to the circuit, then proceed to the next circuit.

9 If the rotor is moving, then use masking tape to mark the faulty circuit. Turn off power to the circuit, then proceed to the next circuit.

10 If circuit contains three-way or four-way switches, flip the lever on each switch individually, and watch for rotor movement after each flip of a switch.

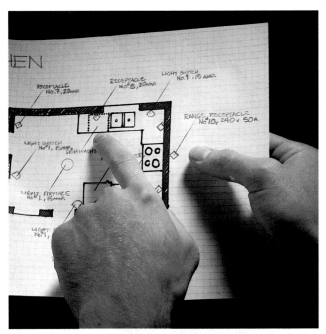

11 For each faulty circuit, identify the appliances, lights, switches, receptacles, and electrical junction boxes powered by the circuit. Use a map of your home wiring system as a guide (pages 30 to 33).

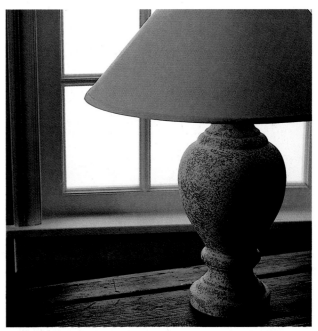

12 Recheck all lights and appliances along each faulty circuit to make sure they are not consuming power. If they are, disconnect them and repeat test.

13 Inspect the electrical boxes along each faulty circuit for dirty wire connections (page 72), damaged wire insulation (page 115), dirt buildup (page 117), or signs of arcing (page 120).

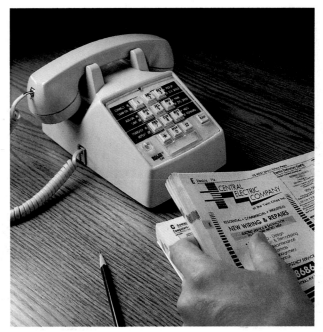

14 If no problems are found in electrical boxes, then the high-resistance short circuit is in wiring contained inside the walls. In this case, consult a licensed electrician.

Index

A

AL-CU wire rating, 22, 44 , 63
Aluminum wire, 21-22, 24
  cleaning, 57, 72
  identifying, 22
  receptacle for, 63
  switches for, 44
American Wire Gauge (AWG) system, 21
Amp, *see:* Ampere
Amperage,
  definition, 6
Amperage rating,
  of appliances, 34-35
  of circuits, 26-28, 32
  of receptacles, 63, 66
  of switches, 44
Ampere, definition, 7
Appliances,
  amperage ratings, 34-35
  circuits, 10-11, 27-28
  common problems, 43, 63
  electrical demand, 34-35
  extension cords for, 119
  fuses, 27-28
  plugs, 94
  receptacles for, 66, 68
  split-circuit wiring for, 64-65
  voltage, 10
  wattage ratings, 34-35
  wire size, 21
Arcing, 38, 62, 116, 120, 122
Armored cable, 17, 20, 64, 84, 115
  definition, 7
Automatic switch, 51, 55

B

Black wire, *see:* Hot wire
Blown fuse, replacing, 29
  see also: Fuse
Box, *see:* Electrical box
Breaker box, 13, 27
  see also: Service panel
Building codes, *see:* Codes
Built-in light fixture switch, 78-79
  testing and replacing, 81
Buried wire, *see:* Underground feeder cable
BX cable, *see:* Armored cable

C

Cable,
  anchoring, 112
  common problems, 112-113
  definition, 7, 21
  stripping, 23
  types, 7, 17, 20-22
Cable clamp, 36, 39, 113
Cable ripper, 19, 23
Cable sheathing, 20-21, 39
Cable splice, 36-37
  installing electrical box, 38-39
Cartridge fuse, *see:* Fuse
Ceiling fixture, 78-79
  box for, 36

common problems, 79
  see also: Light fixture
Chandelier, 78-79, 86-87
Circuit, 14
  definition, 7
  diagram, 14-15
  evaluating for safe capacity, 34-35
  mapping, 8, 30-33, 76
  overloading, 26, 28-29, 34, 63
  shutting off power, 26-27
Circuit breaker, 26-29
  as safety device, 10, 13-14, 26
  definition, 7
  illustration, 14, 29
  resetting, 29
  tripped circuit breaker, 28-29
  types, 28
Circuit breaker panel, *see:* Service panel
Circuit map, 30-33
Circuit tester, *see:* Neon circuit tester
CO/ALR wire rating, 22, 44, 63
Codes (building and electrical), 5, 9, 13, 64,
  74, 79, 110
  inspection wiring, 110-121
Color-coding of wires, 14, 21
Combination tool, 18
Common screw terminal, 46, 53, 58
Conductor, definition, 7
Conduit, 20
  definition, 7
  metal, 17, 20-21, 64
Connecting wires,
  pigtailing, 25
  push-in fittings, 24
  screw terminals, 24
  wire nuts, 25
Continuity,
  definition, 7
  testing for, 52-55
Continuity tester, 18
Copper wire, 21
  as conductor, 21
  as grounding wire, 11-12, 14, 17, 20-21
  cleaning, 57, 72
  receptacle for, 63
  switch for, 44
Current, 16
  definition, 7
  diagram of current flow, 6
  leaks, 122
  measuring, 19
  normal current flow, diagram, 16
  short-circuited current, diagram, 16

D

Demand, *see:* Power demand
Dimmer switch, 60-61
Doorbell,
  cleaning chime plungers, 99
  common problems, 96
  diagram of system, 96
  fixing and replacing, 96-101
  replacing chime unit, 100-101
  replacing switch, 100
  testing, 97-99
  transformer for, 96-98
Double switch, 48, 55
Duplex receptacle,
  definition, 7, 13
  diagram, 63
  repairing and replacing, 72-77
  types, 66-69
  wiring configurations, 64-65
  see also: Receptacle

E

Electric meter, 10-12, 122
  definition, 7
Electrical box,
  and light fixture, 36, 117
  cable for, 113
  cleaning, 117
  code requirements for, 36, 116
  definition, 7, 13
  inspecting, 116-117, 122
  installing, 38-39
  replacing, 40-41
  types, 36-37
Electrical cable, *see:* Cable
Electrical codes, *see:* Codes
Electrical cord, common problems, 118-119
  see also: Plugs
Electrical repairs, tools for, 18-19
Electrical system, 10-11
  diagram, 6, 11-13
  mapping, 30-33
  upgrading, 10-12, 26-27, 37, 65, 74, 79
Electrical tape, 114
Electricity,
  and safety, 8-9
  glossary of terms, 7
  source and supply routes, 10-11
  understanding, 6, 10-15
Electronic motion-sensor switch, 43, 51
Electronic programmable thermostat, 102
  installing, 106
Electronic switch, 51, 55
End-of-run wiring, 64-65, 74
Extension cord, 9, 119

F

Feed wire,
  definition, 7
  identifying, 48-49, 76-77
FHA electrical-service requirements, 26
  see also: Codes
Fixture, *see:* Light fixture
Fluorescent light fixture, 88-93
  ballast, replacing, 92
  common problems, 88-89
  fixture, replacing , 93
  socket, replacing, 91
  starter, replacing, 89
  tube, replacing, 90
Four-way switch, 44, 47
  fixing or replacing, 59
  testing for continuity, 53
Furnace, checking for power, 32
Fuse, 26-29
  as safety device, 10, 13-14, 28
  blown fuse, identifying and replacing, 29
  definition, 7
  how fuses work, 28
  removing, 26-27, 29
  types, 28
Fuse block, 27, 29
Fuse box, *see:* Service panel
Fuse panel, *see:* Service panel
Fuse puller, 19, 29

G

GFCI circuit breaker, 28
  testing, 29
GFCI receptacle, 9, 11, 62, 74
  installing, 75-77